HEROINES OF CHRIST

THE MAID OF ORLEANS, JOAN OF ARC
"A heart of fire, a soldier's soul of steel" — St. Thérèse.

HEROINES
of CHRIST

Edited by

JOSEPH HUSSLEIN, S.J., Ph.D.

St. Louis University

THE BRUCE PUBLISHING COMPANY

Milwaukee

Imprimi potest: P. A. BROOKS, S.J., Praepositus Provincialis,
Prop. Missourianae
Nihil obstat: H. B. RIES, Censor librorum
Imprimatur: ✠ SAMUEL A. STRITCH, Archiepiscopus Milwaukiensis

November 30, 1939

920
Hu

(Third Printing — 1949)

Preface by the Editor

PERHAPS I can best begin this Preface by stating my belief that no dull spot is likely to be found in this book. It is dramatic, vivacious, shot through with light and color, and animated with action.

There is, indeed, no reason why spiritual literature ever should be dull. No prescription exists to that effect. Spirituality itself is the greatest of all possible adventures. There is, in fact, no remotest cause, even, why spiritual persons ever should be prosy, unless it lies within their own personalities. There are no such personalities in this volume.

True, there is prose in every life. But, there is at the same time more true poetry and adventure in the life of God's own saints, than can well be found anywhere else.

I have said that no dull spot is likely to be found in this book. But neither is there any dull spot in the Gospel story. There is no dull spot in the teachings of our Lord, who loved to tell stories weighted with precious meaning — we call them parables — and through them to convey the lessons He had come to impart. "And with many such parables He spoke to them, according as they were able to hear. And without parables He did not speak unto them" (Mark 4:33, 34). And immediately the Evangelist adds, "but apart, He explained all things to His disciples."

He made spiritual truths interesting, attractive, concrete. He made them visible and tangible to men. We need but

2621

here recall the popular figures of the Good Shepherd, the Prodigal Son, the Publican, and the Pharisee. Or we can turn to behold Lazarus, in the bosom of his father Abraham, and Dives in the pit of hell, begging for a drop of water on the finger's tip of the man who had desired no more than the crumbs from the sick man's table, and no one gave them to him as he lay at the gilded gates, his only friends the dogs that licked his sores. There, in brief, is a lesson in practical sociology, vivid, modern, better than a thousand textbooks on the subject.

As for the beautiful legends of some of our early saints, they may well be considered as the poetry of Christianity. What matter if we cannot trace them back to contemporary sources. They are profoundly true and real in the lessons they convey, in the confidence they inspire, in the courage they infuse. They hearten us for Catholic action and for sacrifice. They bring us nearer to our Lord Crucified. Let us thank God for them!

But exactness and historical accuracy have been the rules followed in the writing of the lives presented here. In only a few instances could the entire story not be sufficiently verified. The exceptions are those precisely that have just been indicated. They concern the earlier centuries, where, if not always in so many words, it was made sufficiently clear that the legends and traditions of the Christian ages were accepted by the writer as the precious, age-old heirloom of the Church.

In regard to modern saints, it is often possible to know them more intimately than we can know the members of our own household.

Yet, the writers of this book, members of the Society of

Jesus, are not literalists. They have no hesitation to dramatize events conformably with historic fact, to use the natural language of the heart in order to express the sentiments it deeply cherishes, and to give historic certainties a consistent local coloring and atmosphere. In a word, they have made visible and tangible what else would have remained abstract or undefined. It is what the Church urges us to do in displaying her interest in the cinema, as utilized in the cause of Christ. Precisely some such effort has been made in not a few of the lives here flashed before us in quick, successive pictures.

JOSEPH HUSSLEIN, S.J., PH.D.

Feast of Our Lady of the Way

Contents

CONTENTS

HEROINES OF CHRIST

1

Christ's Passionflower

AGNES

A JOSTLING, shrilling and impatient crowd was packed closely along either side of the Via Juliana, the busy street which led from the headquarters of the Prefect of Rome to the Agonale Circus. It was a holiday throng and the air was dense with a bedlam of voices. But through the shouts and cries ran a note that well might make a stranger's blood run chill.

There was a savagery about this crowd such as one was accustomed to find at the amphitheater when one bloody gladiator had his opponent helpless at his feet, and with sword arm poised, looked to the shrieking gallery for the sign to plunge the ghastly blade home. There was a sickening, lustful note about their shouts, such as one might hear at the theater where shameless plays pandered to the basest passions in the human breast. The crowd was waiting, waiting for a parade to pass by.

That morning the public criers had announced that an unusual spectacle was in store for the people of Rome. Instead of the careening thrills of a chariot race in the Circus Maximus, replacing the boring single combat of slaves, armed with short, razor-sharp swords, in substitution of the thrills that only brought ennui to Rome's jaded populace, a new amusement was to be provided. A young Roman girl of patrician birth was to be punished for the unpardonable crime of being a Christian. But — so the tongues wagged away — the circumstances of her case made it quite extraordinary. Her manner of punishment, too, was unusual. Interest was fanned to a white heat by the report that the son of the Prefect of Rome was intimately concerned in this affair. Further questioning revealed the fact that the young Christian woman, Agnes, had rejected the passionate avowal of love and marriage proposal of the youthful Procopius. Procopius had been smitten with love at first sight of Agnes. He had seen her one day on the streets of Rome and had determined on the spot to have her for his wife.

Because of her determined and persistent refusal to marry the young pagan, and because she openly flaunted her adherence to the hated and despised Christian sect, she had been condemned to a fate that was degrading to her noble rank and shameful to her professed religion. She was to be disgraced in her maidenhood and led down the open street between gaping crowds. A crier was to go before her proclaiming that she, Agnes, had blasphemed the gods and was condemned to a life of shame in punishment. Small wonder the streets of Rome were lined — but with what sort of people?

Along about the year A.D. 289, while Diocletian governed the Roman Empire in the East and Maximian in the West, there was born into the famous old Roman family, the *Gens Claudia,* a child who was named Agnes. Her parents held a place of honor in Roman society. They were, however, remarkable for this that they were not affected by the vices that were rampant in the social order of their day. They were rich, but they did not pamper themselves with Oriental luxuries, as was the general custom. They were powerful, but were content to be unassertive. They owned a large household of slaves, but they did not treat them as animals to be beaten or worked to death; on the contrary, their slaves held more the status of sons and daughters. They were not proud and haughty Romans; they were of lofty moral character and sincere virtue; they were, though secretly, fervent and practical Christians.

Agnes was a beautiful child. She grew to young womanhood remarkable for her beauty of face and form, and for her beauty of character. From her earliest years she was drawn with magnetic force to Christ, whom she came to know with a deep, personal familiarity at an early age. Her vivacity was not in the least bit dampened by the fact that the consuming interest of her life was to love and serve Him alone.

This little maid would often leave her elders gasping with astonishment at the gravity of her statements and the mature wisdom she expressed, both in her opinions and in her conduct. Although she was high strung and impulsive, there was a habitual gentleness and unselfishness about her that spontaneously captivated the hearts of all who knew her.

Agnes, like other Christian children of her day, learned to know Christ in the midst of a persecution that left the Roman soil continually crimsoned with the blood of martyrs. While still a tiny baby, as her nurse would often tell her in later years, she had been carried in the arms of her mother, in the dead of night, to the secret meeting places of the

Christians — now it might be to some rendezvous hidden in the earth beneath some fallen ruins, called the catacombs, or again, the hidden path would lead to the house of a Christian outside the city walls. And always the purpose of these nocturnal visits was that they might assist at the sacred mysteries of the Holy Sacrifice of the Mass, and afterwards drink in with beating hearts and eager minds the beautiful, life-giving truths of Christianity.

Even as a babe, Agnes had been held tight in the embrace of the King whom she was to love so passionately, and for whom she would eventually surrender her life. For the white-robed priest would often place a tiny piece of the consecrated host, Christ's Sacred Body, on her tongue, and would hold to her baby lips the consecrated chalice that she might sip a few drops of the Blood which the Lamb of God — the *Agnus Dei* — whose name she bore, had shed to save mankind.

Never would she forget the anguish her family endured when the rough soldiers had come and dragged off to prison their young Cornelia, a slave girl of her mother's apartments, for being a Christian. They had to stand helplessly by and see her broken on the rack without being able to come to her assistance. How long would this noble Roman family escape the prying eyes of the paid informers? How long would it be before they, too, would be summoned before the tribunal and required either to burn incense before the pagan gods, or lose their property, their social position, and their lives?

God protected them, however, and Agnes' infancy and childhood were spent in the peaceful, though secret, practice of the Christian religion. She received instruction in her faith, both at the hands of her mother, and, along with other boys and girls of her own age, at unsuspected meeting places, from the priests. Agnes' family, like other wealthy Romans, had an educated slave who acted as private tutor. Hence no suspicion was aroused when the education of the girl was carried on within her own home. There was this difference between the slave tutor of Agnes and others at Rome: hers was a fervent Christian. Not only did he ably continue the work of implanting the knowledge and love of Christ and His Church in the heart and mind of the girl, as begun by her parents, but he would also accompany her to the different places where the holy priests were hidden, that she might sit at their feet and learn from them of God and His dearly beloved Son, Christ Jesus.

Agnes was now a beautiful girl of fourteen, in the first blossom of her womanhood. One day she was returning alone from her lessons at the house of a Christian teacher. Paulinus, her slave tutor and trusted companion, had left her to make a purchase at the vegetable market near the Temple of Diana. As Agnes was walking along the Vicus Martius, a small body of horsemen turned into the street fifty yards or so ahead of her and came clattering down the cobblestones at a full gallop. The street was not very broad and there was no sidewalk so Agnes had to jump for her life into a doorway, barely in time to escape the flying hooves of the horses. As the riders flashed past the young woman saw that they were wealthy young Romans, apparently seeking a thrill by their breakneck ride — probably under the influence of the strong Falernian wine. The youthful rider leading the plunging cavalcade caught a glimpse of Agnes as he sped by within a few feet of her. He immediately sawed at the reins and tried to pull his horse to a stop. But the speed and impetus of his ride, along with the unwillingness of his charger to give up the race, had carried him well down the street. By the time he wheeled his horse and cantered back to the spot where Agnes had been pressed into the doorway, she was nowhere in sight. The rider plied spurs to the horse and galloped to the intersection just ahead. He looked to the right — no one in sight but a fruit vendor and an old woman carrying a water jug; he turned to the left just in time to see the one he was seeking enter a lane that led to a large and beautiful home. Musing to himself: "Who can she be, I wonder?" he trotted his mount to the house of the *Gens Claudia*.

"Hold on!" he called to a man who was just passing through the gateway, "do you know who lives here?"

"Yes. The Claudian family."

"Is there a young woman whose face is as fair as that of a goddess, and whose form is as delicate and graceful as a woodland nymph?"

"Why, that must be my young mistress Agnes whom you mean," the slave replied.

Tossing him a coin and a brief word of thanks, the youth pulled the head of his steed round and sped off down the road, a strange light burning in his eyes.

The next day, and for several days after that, the young man waited at a spot near Agnes' home for another glimpse of her. Finally his patience was rewarded. Agnes and her companion, Paulinus, came out of the house and turned down the Via Numentina, in the direction of the sentinel. Now it was his turn to step back into the duck of a doorway. His eyes were enthralled by the beauty of the young woman. Neither she nor her companion were conscious that they were being observed, but proceeded, talking and laughing merrily, on their way. The youthful watcher did not follow them. He stood there for a long time, thinking: "Jove, how beautiful she is." His heart throbbed violently in his breast.

"Love at first sight." The young man's name was Procopius. His name was announced one day, not long after this, to the parents of Agnes, and he was ushered into their presence. "I have come," he said, "to ask the hand of your daughter in marriage." Having spoken these words, he commanded the slaves who accompanied him to deposit at their feet the rich presents he had brought to win for his suit a favorable reception. The gifts were rich spices and delicate Oriental silks, pearls, wispy veils, and even some furs, taken, he said, from the Northern barbarians. Begging Agnes' parents to look with favor upon him as a future son-in-law, he told them that he, too, was of high social rank, and that his father was Symphronius, the Prefect of Rome. A more advantageous betrothal than this could hardly have been arranged, even had they planned and contrived with all their might to bring it about.

Sadly Agnes' mother and father faced each other when the young man had gone. "There is nothing to do but tell Agnes, and let her decide whether she will have Procopius for a husband," said her father.

"You know she won't," quietly rejoined his wife. "Procopius is a pagan."

"Yes," he replied, "I know that; and I know what Agnes' answer will be. Are you ready, my dear, to pay the price that will be demanded of us?"

"Yes," she answered in a low voice.

Agnes refused every advance of the young Roman. At first he had thought that it was coyness on her part, and had refused to be put off. But now he was certain of one thing: she did not want anything to do with him. Next he had prevailed upon influential relatives and friends to come and plead his cause. They promised Agnes riches, a palace, country estates, numerous slaves — in short, all the delightful things of life if she would consent to marry Procopius. Her refusal remained adamant; her *no* was unchanged.

Once again the young man came to her to plead his love, laying at her feet more precious gifts. Agnes was alarmed at the vehemence of his passion, and the burning words he uttered.

"No," she said, "you must go. You must never see me again. For already a lover has secured my heart. He has given me ornaments more precious than yours, and has placed His ring upon my finger as a pledge of fidelity. He has adorned my arms with priceless bracelets, and has enriched my neck with diamonds as dazzling as the springtime sun. My Beloved has placed His right hand on my forehead, that I may know no lover but Himself."

The young pagan looked at her with jealousy smoldering in his eyes, and hatred raging in his breast. He could not understand that Agnes meant her Divine Lover, and that the precious ornaments she named signified the spiritual treasures of grace with which her soul had been enriched by Baptism and the other Sacraments, and which Jesus Christ promised to increase still further in reward for her virginity.

"Who is this lover?" Procopius insisted. "I don't believe you have a lover at all."

"Oh, but I have," Agnes assured him. "And He is more powerful, more noble, His countenance more charming in my eyes, His love sweeter to my heart, His presence more delightful, than anything in the world. His voice enchants my ears like a beautiful melody; His beauty is such that the sun and stars are aghast at it. His ministers are angels; His soldiers are armed with swords of flame. At His touch the sick are healed; the dead awaken at His word. His resources never fail; His riches are never exhausted. I have pledged my faith. I have vowed to be entirely His. I can love Him and remain chaste, press Him to my heart and still be pure, receive Him as my Lover and still be a virgin."

Procopius, disappointed, miserable, departed with a gleam of madness in his eyes.

Love rejected affects different temperaments in different ways. For some it merely whets their eagerness to win the object of their desire. There is, however, one element that seems to be common to the majority of those who are disappointed in love: bitterness, unhappiness, gnawing dissatisfaction with everything in life possesses them. Such was the case with the love-sick Procopius. The physicians in consultatation decided that the only cure for him lay in the possession of his heart's desire. Thus it happened that the Prefect came in person to see if Agnes would not reconsider the proposal of his son. Once again she refused. Nothing in the world could make her violate her vowed fidelity to her first love. Symphronius insisted that a more illustrious husband could nowhere be found. Was he not the son of the first man in Rome? This, however, meant nothing to Agnes. When he had left the young woman, the Prefect made careful inquiries who this mysterious lover of hers might be. One of his secret-service agents entered breathlessly to announce that he had excellent proof that the young woman was a Christian, and that this lover of hers was the God of the Christians, Jesus Christ, the Nazarene.

The Prefect was overjoyed at hearing this. He would summon Agnes before his tribunal; he was sure that he now had the solution to this trying situation. He knew that he held her fate in the palm of his hand.

No one dared appear to defend a person arraigned on the charge of being a Christian. Besides, as he soon found out, a defense lawyer was superfluous, since Agnes, far from denying her affiliations with Christianity, or maintaining an attitude of silence and requiring the state to prove its case against her, stated simply that she was a Christian, and had been all her life. Symphronius smiled indulgently at the fair, young defendant. He would be the friend rather than the judge; he would win her over with honeyed words rather than harsh, menacing ones. But Agnes remained unshaken. Persuasion failing, the Prefect's manner abruptly changed; a mocking smile on his lips and a cold gleam in his eyes, he asked:

"Well, my dear, do you think you would like the sharp teeth of a hungry leopard in your throat? Or would you prefer to have your delicate limbs mangled and broken on the wheel?"

Agnes only smiled, an undaunted smile. Flatteries or threats, it made no difference to this fearless girl. But the Prefect had another card to play. This one would not fail to break her spirit. He would, he told her, ruin her parents. They were of the nobility, it is true, and hence he could not employ violence against them. But there was a more subtle and deadly way to bring about their downfall. If she did not repudiate her Christianity and marry his son, he would accuse them before the assembly of being Christians. In the face of such a charge — unrefuted, as it would be — all the privileges of rank, even the title of citizen, were dissolved, property and wealth were confiscated, exile or death was the end. For the Christian there was but one law — that of *proscription*. With these words ringing in her ears, he ordered Agnes to be locked in a prison cell so that she might think over his alternative during the night. Next day she was brought before him again. She was unshaken.

"All right, give her another night to consider." For the third time she appeared before him, and with more firmness than ever she refused to abjure her Faith or her lover, Christ.

"If you are determined to be a virgin," said the Prefect, "you shall be one. But . . . it is a Vestal virgin you shall be. You are going to be consecrated to the goddess Vesta; you will spend the rest of your life replenishing the sacred fire at her altars."

The undaunted Agnes replied: "If for the love of Jesus Christ I have refused to marry your son, who, for all his unreasoning and undesired love for me, is at least a living man, how could I vow to serve a lifeless idol? How could I sin against the God of heaven and earth by bowing my head before a piece of stone?"

"Take your choice between sacrificing to the goddess Vesta, along with the other virgins consecrated to her service, or being consigned to a state of lasting disgrace. You laugh at the threat of punishment, even the losing of your life, but there may be worse things still than that to fear."

"You are," continued the Prefect, "a young woman of common sense. Do you want to sacrifice to Vesta and save the honor of your family, or do you wish to shame your parents by becoming an object of public scorn?"

"Christ does not abandon His own," Agnes told her persecutor, "He will never permit the modesty consecrated to Him to be defiled. You may stain your sword with my blood, but you cannot stain my body with uncleanness. I know the power of Jesus Christ. I trust in Him; I despise your threats. I shall neither sacrifice to Vesta, nor will my body suffer harm, for the Lord has placed His angel near me to protect me."

The Prefect motioned to several of his soldiers to approach the young woman and delivered her over to their rough hands to prepare her for the dolorous march to the Agonale Circus. For this, with all the accumulated mental and physical horrors of that place, was to be her destination. "You, there," he called to another soldier, "will walk ahead of them proclaiming that this woman is a Christian who has blasphemed the gods, and is condemned to the *Lupanar*."

God in His wisdom permitted her modesty to be painfully tried, as was that of the Divine Lamb of God, for whom she herself was named Agnes, the "lamb." But by His power He saved her from the unhallowed gaze of lewd eyes. Her golden hair fell loose to cover and envelop her, and His love went with her as she was led out on her Via Dolorosa, between the waiting crowds, on to the Agonale Circus. As she passed through the coarse, unruly crowd, with vice written boldly on the features of many, did they cry out and jeer at her? Or was there something that held them bound as they looked into the upturned face, lit, as it were, with the light of

Heaven? Could they gaze untouched into the wonder of that countenance, with its beauty of virginal innocence.

But Christ was with His bride, and His love could not fail her. Her heart, though it throbbed within her breast, disdained to know fear.

When the little cortege reached its destination an angel of the Lord awaited Agnes to protect her. No one dared approach this fearless girl. Many were struck with astonishment at her self-possession, and were convinced in their hearts that the God of the Christians was the true God.

Suddenly there was an excited flurry on the outskirts of the crowd and a flushed youth shouldered his way through, to the spot where Agnes stood. Cursing those standing around for being cowards, he strode toward the girl, intending to seize her. A quick gasp ran through the crowd watching the young man. They saw him reach out his hand, stop, stand for a few tense seconds staring with terrified countenance at something they could not see, then pitch forward with his face to the earth; the prostrate body quivered slightly, then, was motionless. Agnes' protecting angel had struck him dead.

Meanwhile, the crowd grew larger and more unruly. Voices were raised: "She is a sorceress. She killed the Prefect's son. Stone her to death." Others took up the cry. Some few protested: "No. She is an innocent girl. Let her go free."

The Prefect, on learning what had happened to his son, hurried to the *Lupanar*. When he saw the motionless body he threw himself down beside it with a heart-rending cry. When the first gust of grief subsided he turned to Agnes:

"I beg you, restore my son to life. I will believe that you have not killed him by sorcery if you will do so."

"Your faith is not deserving of such a miracle," Agnes told him, "but to show forth the divine power of Jesus Christ I will ask Him to restore the life of your son." She prayed. Soon the young man began to breathe, gaspingly at first, then rhythmically. In a short time he sat up and looked about. His eyes shone as though he had seen a wonderful vision. "There is but one God in heaven, on earth, and in the whole universe," he cried out. "He is the God of the Christians. All our temples are meaningless; our gods are mere stone and wood, who are powerless to help us." Symphronius, the Prefect, and many other spectators were also converted by this miracle to believe in Jesus Christ.

However, there was an even greater number, who at the urging of the pagan priests, shouted out: "Seize the sorceress. Away with her." Symphronius, lacking the courage to refuse the shrieking mob its prey, surrendered the matter to his lieutenant, Aspasius, a violent pagan. Aspasius was not slow to play to the gallery, especially since he himself had no love for the Christians. He commanded that a large fire be lighted in the *Forum Boarium,* and Agnes be thrown into it. When this order was carried out the flames divided into two parts, leaving her untouched, and darting out on either side, burned those who were standing near.

Aspasius was now hard put to satisfy those who demanded the death of the young woman. He was trembling with fear at the marvels of divine power he had twice witnessed; he feared that any further contrivances of his might backfire upon himself. He also feared the mob, whose fury was growing out of bounds. Urged on by the rabble leaders it surged toward him. "She shall be beheaded," Aspasius shouted. "She shall die by the sword." The mob was satisfied.

The executioner, sword in hand, approached the smiling maiden. Lifting her eyes to heaven, she said: "Christ Jesus, draw my soul to Thyself." The executioner had had much experience at this sort of work, but now his arm became weak and he stood trembling before this unwavering slip of a girl — he appeared to be the one condemned. She smiled, spoke a reassuring word to him, and he was heartened to perform his task. With a single stroke he severed her head from her body. Angels bore her pure soul to the Lover who awaited her. Holding her in His embrace, He crowned her with a twofold crown: the brilliant diadems of martyrdom and virginity.

Heroism has always made its appeal to the human heart. We love physical courage: courage that does not flinch in the face of threatening danger. But even more admirable — though not so loudly celebrated — is moral courage. The number of moral heroes and heroines who daily fight the good fight, who resist the most seductive allurements to sin, who face the foes that assail them tooth and nail, without yielding an inch, may never have their deeds of heroism portrayed in song or story — or by the modern means of propaganda, the newspaper and motion pictures, but, nevertheless, they are noble, intrepid characters who deserve the splendid awards of heroism.

And their reward shall not be withheld, from them whether, like Agnes, their statues arise over thousands of altars in years to come, or they be crowned amid the company of angels and saints alone, by the hand of Christ in His Celestial Paradise, with Mary at their side.

Yet the glory of Agnes upon earth, since the early centuries of the Church, has been for men's own inspiration, encouragement, and delight, that they might imitate her high ideals, draw strength from her very frailty in which God could work such wonders of courage through her cooperation with His grace, and be purified by the loveliness of her ever virginal purity.

For sixteen centuries now the memory of this child maiden has remained enshrined in the heart of Christendom, a lily in the first beauty of its opening bloom, pearled with the red dew of martyrdom. Deeds wrought to win renown have been forgotten like grass that withers in the sun, but each day on hundreds of thousands of altars, in lofty cathedral or jungle hut, wherever the Divine Lamb of God is mystically immolated on the altar, the name of Agnes, His little "lamb," who shared with Him His Passion and Death, is sweetly commemorated in the solemn Canon of the Mass. Over all the world artists have rivaled each other to present for us anew, in poetry and painting, song and sculpture, this young woman of Rome, who was so fearless, so calm and unflinching in facing tortures and death for her high principles and her Divine Lover. A young heart can understand and appreciate the spirit that animated Agnes, and is fortified at the memory to cling tighter to his or her own high ideals, to pay any price rather than weakly abandon them. Agnes, a girl of heroic caliber, is a model for the youth of every era of history, especially our own, when a new spirit of paganism, much like that of her own Rome, has taken root in America. She stands before us, this beautiful little heroine, this Passionflower of the Divine Lover.

2

Mary of Light

MARIA DE LA LUZ CAMACHO

THE heavy theater curtains sweep together, and the last act is over. A thunderous crescendo of applause greets the heroine as she steps again before the footlights, curtseying deeply, and smiling acknowledgment of the ovation. Her cheeks are still flushed, her eyes shining. She has not yet slipped back to reality. She is still Myriam, the martyr, and in her heart keep ringing those last lines . . . "Jesus! if such delights . . . can with death be mingled . . . let me die now . . . let me die . . ."

An hour later, Maria de la Luz Camacho and her father are speeding down one of Mexico City's beautiful boulevards. They stop for a traffic light. . . . Señor Camacho glances at the fine profile of his daughter outlined against the faint crimson glow from the signal. . . . He wonders why she is so pensive.

"Your acting was superb," he ventures. "The first thing I know you'll be in Hollywood."

Maria de la Luz, with a little start, laughingly replies, "Did you ever know anyone in Hollywood to play parts like mine . . . parts so beautiful?"

Maria de la Luz Camacho was born in Mexico City on May 17, 1907. Twenty-seven years later she was to die a glorious and heroic death on the very threshold of the parish church with those words upon her martyr lips immortalized by a throng of other Mexican Catholic heroes: "Long live Christ the King."

Maria de la Luz was named after the Queen and Patroness of Mexico under the title of Our Lady of Light. Mexico at the time of her birth and early childhood was enjoying the pleasant calm that precedes a storm. Maria attended a convent school at Tlalpan. Her stay here was a brief one, and in July, 1918, she returned to Mexico City, where she entered a private school patronized by the best families of the district. Here her engaging smile and personality made her a dynamo which generated energetic student activity. Her enthusiasm fired her companions to emulate her. The result was that especially the dramatic life of the school was given an impetus because of her passionate love for the theater. She thrilled them with her Joan of Arc and Mary of Scotland.

Eighty pairs of enraptured brown eyes would follow her every movement, and, when the performance was ended, acclaim her "the best actress that ever lived!"

Maria de la Luz fostered this talent which was later on to prove an invaluable means of furthering Catholic Action.

On July 31, 1926, public worship was prohibited in all churches of Mexico. Catholic life, however, responded with an increase of loyalty and devotion.

"My priests are in hiding. My tabernacles are empty. I am shrouded in sorrow," was the cry of Mexico's heart.

In this critical period for Catholicism in Mexico, a wonderful apostolate sprang up to nourish and preserve Catholic life. An army of catechists, enrolled chiefly from the well-to-do families, animated by the loftiest of supernatural ideals, carried on, as far as they could, the work of their hunted priests.

Maria de la Luz at once took a leading part in this work. Teas, parties, and the other distractions of the younger set were insignificant trifles in the face of this opportunity of fighting for Christ. It was not long before her quick intelligence, tact, and zeal, along with her genius for leadership were recognized, and she was made first, Secretary, then Treasurer, of the *Centre General*. "Christ the King! Long live Christ the King," is the watchword that Pius XI gave to the Catholics of Mexico. These words were on her lips all the time. They formed the theme of the plays she wrote, of the songs she taught the children. These were to be her dying words — her legacy to the young soldiers of Catholic Action.

The Camacho home is ablaze with lights. It is the night of Maria de la Luz's party. Across the patio come the sounds of intermingled music and laughter. Gay young couples have been arriving for the past hour. Maria, looking charming in white, receives each guest and interchanges a few happy words. Never was a debutante at her coming-out party more excited, more starry eyed, than Maria de la Luz tonight. Unlike a debutante, however, she has not made her home lovely with flowers to impress social acquaintances. She has striven only to please one Guest. He would arrive any moment.

In Mexico at this time, it was a crime to assist at Mass or receive Holy Communion. But every enactment Calles promulgated simply made Catholics more determined they should not be deprived of the Body and Blood of their Lord. Private citizens offered the use of their homes, and, under cover of darkness, the priest would come, bringing the Blessed Sacrament for adoration. After midnight, he would say Mass, and all would receive Communion.

The party, then, is simply a ruse to allay suspicion on the part of Government informers. All last night Maria de la Luz was heard murmuring in her sleep:

"Ven a mi . . . Jesus, Jesus, come to me . . ."

How carefully she had arranged the white roses on the little table that was to serve as an altar. Her father coming upon her that afternoon had to smile. Perfume atomizer in hand, she was trying to heighten the fragrance of the flowers that were to welcome her King.

One might think this incident somewhat sentimental, but for just such an act — foolish though it seemed in the eyes of some of the Apostles — Jesus praised Mary of Bethany.

Practical-minded, twentieth-century Americans with their Puritan background are inclined to look askance at the devotional practices of Catholic countries like Spain and Mexico. It must be admitted that religion adds color and romance to their lives which are lacking in our own.

For example, it is the beautiful custom in Mexico for a young lover on the birthday of his fiancée to come before dawn to her window and serenade her with a love song that his father and grandfather have sung before him. This traditional melody of haunting sweetness has been adapted and is sung in honor of Mary of Guadalupe by thousands of young men on her feast day. It is truly inspiring to see them coming before daylight, with blue lanterns in their hands, singing to the accompaniment of guitars and tambourines.

Maria de la Luz shuddered. Once more her glance swept over the lurid advertisements in front of the movie house.

"We'll soon stop that," was her low-voiced comment to her companions.

"Take these handbills and give one to every person you meet. I'll take my post outside the theater. Four of you stand on the street corners, and the rest of you distribute your bills to the homes in this district."

Maria de la Luz was protesting against an immoral picture being shown at a prominent theater in Mexico City. She had called her assistants together and given them handbills of protest she had had printed.

"But Maria," argued Carmen Riez, "what if some of those brutal Communists see us and beat us and drag us off to jail? You know, Maria, they have done so for less than this."

"Carmen," said Maria, "haven't you got a Guardian Angel? Ask him to protect you. We shouldn't be afraid to brave some danger for Christ the King."

As the girls hurried down the street, they heard the theater manager shouting at Maria de la Luz:

"Get away from here, you contemptible little meddler!"

As is frequently the case with attractive and talented girls, Maria had to endure the carping criticism and snubbing of jealous friends. God had undoubtedly given her unusual gifts and she developed and used them to the utmost in His service. Her personality and leadership dominated every activity in which she participated. Success attended her efforts. Soon she was accused of monopolizing the limelight, and, as a result, she met with coldness. At times, her life became tragically lonely.

Maria de la Luz felt this deeply, but not a word of complaint crossed her lips. She smiled bravely and continued to do her best. At times, when someone had been particularly cruel, she would go to her room when she returned home, throw herself on the bed and weep bitterly. But in a short time she would be herself again, as serene as ever on the exterior, and no one would guess her anguish.

"Why make others suffer," she would say, "when we can bear our burdens alone?"

To her father confessor, however, she would unburden her heart. She told him of the pain she suffered from her envious companions. She found excuses for them and forgave them from her heart. When her best friend deserted her, this was almost the last straw. Disconsolate, she fled to her spiritual director for guidance. He said:

"Perhaps our Lord has allowed you to lose your friend that He may take entire possession of your heart."

Reflecting upon these words, she went directly to the Church, and there, before the Blessed Sacrament, she surrendered to Jesus her heart, and offered the sacrifice of *all* human friendship if He so wished it.

"I'm afraid we're in for it again," was the greeting of Señor Camacho one evening.

Maria de la Luz who had been awaiting his arrival could tell by the seriousness of his manner that another storm of persecution was about to break.

His prophecy proved correct. From midsummer of 1934, the Catholics were in constant danger. The new reign of terror was inaugurated by Homero Margalli and his relative Garrido Canabal, the "big boss" of Mexico City. They frankly intended that life for the Catholics, which for the past ten years had been no bed of roses, should now be made insupportable.

Margalli tried to make it look as if he and his Reds were the victims of persecution, claiming that the Catholics insulted them and disturbed their meetings by ringing the church bells.

This state of affairs necessitated Maria de la Luz's discontinuation of her catechetical work. A police raid would have meant the ruin of her family. In October of the same year, the house of Madame Solana de Ituarte was raided and four young Catholic girls dragged off to some unknown punishment. Through all this sort of horror, the loyalty and courage of the Mexican people has been almost unbelievable.

The surprise party that Margalli had prepared for December 30, was not wholly unexpected. The Reds had been becoming more and more arrogant.

Down the street was heard the roar of voices. Homero Margalli smiled. In a few seconds his sixty stout lads would be lined up before him. Only Centenario Park lay between the Town Hall and the Catholic church. They could easily set out from the Town Hall, proceed through the park, rush upon the church, and, after they had fired the ten rounds of ammunition he was providing for each, hurry back to the Town Hall where he would welcome them. It was Sunday. He was going to teach these Catholics a lesson they wouldn't forget.

Margalli saluted the red-and-black-uniformed youths as they drew up in front of the Town Hall. They were in high spirits, shouting lustily, "Long live the Revolution!" Margalli talked to them, working them up until he could see that they were savage in the intensity with which they cursed and clenched their fists. He assured them of their own personal safety after the matter was accomplished. They had Garrido's promise for that. Each man was provided with a revolver, ammunition, and a swig of good strong whiskey. Thus fortified, they made their way into the park.

Their first move was to drape a red and black flag over the arms of a monumental Mission Cross in the center of the park and affix to it a picture of Margalli. Then one of the soldiers began to harangue them, vehemently denouncing all things Catholic. A youth of fifteen followed, winning cheers for his vitriolic speech:

"The Liberator of Tabasco has set us a glorious example which we must follow. Religion is our enemy, and we must get rid of it, by killing all the priests, by burning holy images and all churches. We count on the support of the Government which looks upon our determination with sympathy and it is ready to give us a helping hand. The President of the Republic is powerless to prevent us, for Garrido, and not he, is the real ruler of Mexico City!"

"The Reds are going to burn the church!"

The cry circulated like wildfire. Maria de la Luz's thoughts flew at once to the two hundred children now at Mass. She made up her mind. Putting on a green silk sport dress with a white satin collar, she set out with her younger sister Lupita.

"Why are you all dressed up?" her sister inquired.

"When we are going to defend Christ the King," answered Maria de la Luz, "ought we not look our best?"

As they approached the church the orating in the park was

in its last menacing stages. A fierce surge of anger and hatred had swept over the mob.

In the church, Father Rafael Medina was saying the prayers at the foot of the altar:

"I will go unto the altar of God. . . . Because Thou art God my strength . . ."

The great Mass had begun. There was no room for fear. They were climbing Calvary together with Christ. What ineffable honor if some of them were to mount the Cross with Him as Peter and Paul and the other holy martyrs of the Church had done before!

Maria de la Luz took her stand at the church door. If any Red entered, he would do so over her dead body. Lupita was with her.

A youth in a black and red uniform approached the two girls. Maria de la Luz recognized him as a boy she had prepared for First Communion.

"Miss Camacho," he began earnestly, "they are going to burn the church. Please go away!"

Maria de la Luz's eyes took on the old determined look. The boy might just as well have been addressing a stone wall.

When the church bells rang announcing the Elevation, the cries of the mob rose to a pitch that could mean only one thing. They were about to attack. A paralyzing fear gripped those kneeling in the church. Somewhere a revolver cracked. The Celebrant, fearing desecration, hastened to consume the Sacred Species.

Outside Maria de la Luz met the onrush. The young girl's courage facing them alone, daring them to shoot her, compelled their respect. A few began to recede. Others started to move toward her.

"Cursed be Christ the King," someone cried.

"Praised be Christ the King," Maria de la Luz shouted in response.

The Red leader, furious that they should be thwarted by a mere girl, turned to his comrades and shouted:

"Long live the Revolution!" This was the signal to open fire.

"Long live Christ . . ."

Her cry was drowned in a volley of pistol fire.

The lives of Miguel Pro, S.J., and Maria de la Luz are proof that sanctity is not a thing of past ages, but is something as abiding as the Catholic Church itself.

Maria de la Luz, faithful to the name, is a *light* to the Catholic youth of the whole world in the advancement of the modern apostolate: Catholic Action.

3

White Dove of Rome*

CECILIA

ROME, the city of the Emperors, soon after the beginning of the third century of our era, lay bright in the Italian sun. Its gleaming white temples, its stately monuments, its palatial dwelling places, all bespoke the greatness and wealth of the empire. It had begun from nothing, and through military prowess had spread its power across the surface of the earth.

Yes, it was a great empire, and it had seen many great men. But into the story of the Roman emperors is woven, too, a tale of jealousy and hatred, of ignorance and idolatry and bloodshed. Although the empire produced good and just men, yet the monsters of cruelty who controlled its destinies at times, obscured its seeming splendor.

In these palaces lived the emperors and in these temples they sacrificed; but, in the hearts of the poor, in the slums and tenement houses, there had been kindled a small flame which, gathering in strength, was to envelop in its fire the whole of pagan Rome, and ultimately the entire world. That flame was the fire of Christianity!

At the time this story opens the Church of Christ had been at its endless apostolic work for almost two hundred years. The blood of its martyrs had sustained it through

---

* The title is taken from the poem by St. Thérèse of the Child Jesus, "The Melody of St. Cecilia."

cruel persecutions, and it continued constantly to spread and progress so that the voice of its apostles was heard over all the earth.

Persecution and bloodshed are not incredible to us of today. Tyrants and godless governments of the twentieth century have made the cruelty of Roman emperors live anew. Nor is the heroism of martyrs a faroff fact. It is a living reality that makes us shudder at the depths of passion to which men can fall, and at the same time wonder at the lofty heights to which others can attain by the grace of God. The heroism of Christians never fails mankind. It goes on, and is reflected no less in the kindly charity and brotherhood of the truly faithful than in the lifeblood shed by the blessed martyrs themselves.

When we picture, therefore, a young woman of Rome in the beginning of the third century after Christ, stately, beautiful, arrayed in the flowing garments of the Roman aristocracy, going about among the poor of the slums, giving them food and clothing and alms, speaking cheerfully to them and consoling them, it will not be something new to us. Such charity still blossoms in the twentieth century. The story of Cecilia has been told over and over again through the centuries, gaining perhaps a few details here and there, and losing others, so that the legend of her life as we know it cannot be relied upon too much for exactness. Yet behind the legend are the historical facts of her heroism, and we repeat once again the story that has come down to us.

Cecilia was a good and quite literally splendid girl, and at the same time extremely sensible. Her mother, no doubt, was a fervent Christian, but her father had not been gifted with the light of faith. From infancy Cecilia had been trained by her mother in the doctrines of Christianity. She had been taught how to pray, and was told the simple story of Christ, the Son of God. As the light of reason dawned and grew bright in the youthful mind, she realized more and more the beauty of her faith. To her it was something living and real.

We must remember that it was only less than two hundred years before, that Christ had walked upon this very earth, and His life was just as vivid and recent to her and her fellow Christians as that of Washington, for example, is to us. So she took the teaching of Christianity literally. There were the facts confirmed, beyond all possibility of challenge, there were the immortal words of Christ just as He had spoken them. The doctrine of the Mystical Body and of Catholic Action, as we know it today, were taken for granted. It never entered into Cecilia's mind to doubt that all men were her brothers in Christ, that they were all members actually, or had the possibility of becoming members, of the same Mystical Body of which Christ is the head.

So her errands of mercy and consolation to the poorer districts of the city became more and more frequent. She moved among the poor like an angel of goodness, and they loved her. The children, seeing her coming along laden down with bundles, would stop their playing and race to her. She was kind to them, laughed with them, and gave them her welcome gifts.

But one task which she performed was especially dear to her. Gruesome in itself, it was rendered sweet by her love of God and those dear to Him. This was the task of burying the sacred bodies of the martyrs, who had been put to death for their faith, and who for this very reason had a claim above all others to her kindness. It was not an easy task, and it was dangerous. Many times she had to go about by night, in order that she might not be discovered performing these last rites which had been forbidden by the Prefect of the city. Nevertheless, she did it, and found joy in doing it.

All this time, while caring for others, she did not neglect her own soul. Pope Urban I, the seventeenth pontiff to reign on the throne of Peter, had come to know her and rely much upon her in his work. He himself was a marked man. He had to lie in hiding among the tombs of the catacombs, lest he be found out and taken from his flock. But Cecilia, as a noble Roman maiden, could go about more openly. Moreover, because her family was wealthy, she could do much for the poor that he did not find within his means to do. At all events, she came to him often for instruction and spiritual guidance. She assisted at the holy Mass that he celebrated, and from his hands received the Sacred Body and Blood of Christ Himself in Holy Communion. She delighted in reading the Holy Scriptures, finding stored there the treasures of eternal truth. We are told that beneath the costly apparel which nobility was accustomed to wear, she always wore as a mortification, a coarse, rough garment. Then, too, she made it a regular practice to fast several times a week. It was thus that she strengthened and guarded herself against temptation.

For a long time a secret hope and desire had been growing in Cecilia's heart. In her determination to love Christ and Christ alone, she wanted to give herself wholly to Him by consecrating her virginity to God. She debated with herself at length. Marriage and motherhood were among the most beautiful things on earth. Marriage was something sacred, a sacrament instituted by her Lord. Yet she never for a moment doubted that this same Lord was calling her to be the bride of none but Himself. And so, under Urban's guidance, she bound herself by vow to remain a virgin forever. When she had made her promise, she was thrilled and happy as a little child. The honor of being His alone, of belonging to no one but Him, especially in those first moments of realization, brought a new light into her eyes and a new cheerfulness into her daily routine.

And then the inevitable happened! She was strolling through the flower garden one afternoon just at sunset, when a servant came and told her that her mother wished to speak to her. Of itself this was nothing, but there was something important on foot when her mother wished to speak to her in her own private chamber. So Cecilia, wondering what it might be, crossed the portico and entered through the doors.

"You sent for me, Mother?" Cecilia asked, after she had entered her mother's room and found her sitting beside a table with a book of Scripture in her hand. She always liked to see her mother thus, sitting quietly and reading.

"Yes, my daughter, I have something to tell you." The mother looked upon her daughter and again felt the comfort and joy she always experienced when she watched her. This was her own Cecilia, in whom as an infant she had planted the seed of faith and nourished it and watched it grow, until now in its full bloom, it seemed to shine out through her sparkling eyes, reflecting the inward peace and purity of soul that were hers, and accentuating her already radiant loveliness. And now, she thought, how would it all end? "You are grown up now, Cecilia, and you know your father has plans for you."

"Plans, Mother?"

"Yes, dear; he has decided that you are old enough to marry and start a family of your own."

"But Mother, what will all this mean?"

"I know what it will mean to you, Cecilia. I have not forgotten your promise to our Lord. I have lain awake at night, trying to think what we might do, and I have prayed for many weeks. But, it seems, to no avail. Your father is inexorable. We must continue to pray, and I'm sure that God will send us help in some way."

"Mother, is it Valerianus?"

"Yes, dear; it has all been arranged. He is a noble, handsome young man, and he loves you dearly."

"I know, Mother, I know he loves me. I love him, too, but I love him as a brother, because he is so good and kind, and not as one who is to be my husband."

"Yes, dear, I know. But if the Lord wishes to preserve you for Himself alone, He will certainly help us. In the meantime, we must pray and be resigned with what He sends us."

With this, Cecilia left her mother, and with a troubled heart strolled in the twilight through the rose garden. At first she could not imagine what she could do. Valerianus had always loved her, ever since they were children, and she loved him in return — but always as a brother. As the light faded into darkness and the stars appeared one by one in the sky, she began to pray to Mary, the Virgin of virgins. Mary had vowed virginity, too, and to preserve it, she had been willing even to give up the very Motherhood of God. But God had made it possible for her to remain a virgin, and yet become the Mother of Christ. Surely, at her intercession, God would find some way for Cecilia.

Weeks passed, and true to his word, Cecilia's father made definite plans for the marriage. His unbelief and his adamant will made it impossible for Cecilia to reveal to him the secret of her vow. Nor could she tell Valerianus, her husband-to-be. He was overjoyed at the prospect of marrying Cecilia. These days he was much more lighthearted than of old. The laughter and joy that suffused his handsome countenance were quite contagious, as he went about telling all the world of his beautiful bride.

But he could not quite explain that look in Cecilia's eyes. It was puzzling. Even in the midst of all the preparations, during all the gaiety of the days before the great day, that almost sad, yet hopeful, trusting look lingered in her eyes. Perhaps, he thought, she is a bit frightened at leaving her mother and father for a family of her own. Ah, well, he would soon take care of that. Once she was his own, he would make up to her, and more than make up, for what she was sacrificing for him. They two were to be made one, bound together for all their lives, and in the joy of that union, he would make her forget all sadness and sorrow. She would be his and his alone, and nothing but happiness would be theirs.

The day finally arrived, and still none knew the secret but Cecilia and her mother. They talked little of it. Yet merely to glance at each other during the festival was to convey one single idea back and forth between them: the task seems impossible, but the Lord is powerful and good. The feasting went on, and through it all Cecilia was pleasant and agreeable, but far from bubbling over with ecstasy, as Valerianus seemed to be. While the musicians played the nuptial hymns, she sang in her heart to God alone, and that look of blind trust remained in her eyes. Valerianus saw it still, and was puzzled still, but could give himself no better explanation than before. He soon forgot it in the midst of all the wedding celebrations. When, after a long day, the night came and the great torches were lit, the festivities went on and on to the tune of clinking goblets and throbbing lyres and feet flying in the dance.

It was very late when finally Cecilia and Valerianus were brought to the bridal chamber, both of them very tired, and Valerianus, at least, glad to be alone at long last with his bride. But this was the hardest time for Cecilia. Now she must tell him, no matter how much it hurt him. She could do nothing else. As the door closed behind their attendants, the two stood and looked at each other in silence across the room, he, more than ever conscious of the look in her eyes, she perceiving clearly in his eyes his great love for her; she, exceedingly beautiful in her white bridal gown, he, strong and swarthy in the flower of youth. She was the first to speak.

"Valerianus, I have something I must tell you."

"What is it, my own Cecilia?" he asked.

"It is a great and wonderful secret," she replied, "and therefore you must promise me first never to reveal it to anyone."

"I could refuse you nothing, my dear," he answered, "and I give you my solemn word never to tell it to anyone, no matter what I must suffer in keeping it."

"I want you to know," she said, "that I have an angel of God for my friend, who with the greatest zeal guards over my virginity. If you should try to take it from me, he will vent his wrath upon you; but if you love me only with a pure and immaculate love, and join him in guarding over me, he will love you as he does me."

There! She had told him. Relief and hope came to her as she prayed silently and watched him. First there had been incomprehension on his face, then almost anger, then wonder and even fear, as he turned her words over in his mind. At last he spoke:

"Cecilia, if you wish me to believe this, you must show me this angel you speak of." Then, as jealousy and the fear of losing his newly won treasure overwhelmed him, he added, "But if this be not an angel, and only another man, I will kill both you and him."

His passionate words rang through the chamber and died away, almost before he could realize their full import. In the moment of silence that followed, he repented of having spoken them. But Cecilia seemed not to notice.

"Dear Valerianus," she said, "you *can* see the angel; but first you must be cleansed in the eternal waters of regeneration, and believe in the one true God of the Christians."

Eagerly he replied, "I will do anything, Cecilia. I will believe. Only tell me what I must do."

"You must go to a holy old man called Urban, Valerianus. He will instruct you and cleanse you in the waters of Baptism. Take the Appian Way as it leaves the city, and go to the third milestone. There you will find the poor who beg their livelihood from passersby. They are my friends and know my secret. They will take you to Urban, if you but say: 'Cecilia sent me to you, so that you may take me to Urban; I have a message from her to him.' Then when you see him, tell him all that has passed between us, and of my promise to you. After he has instructed and baptized you, return to me here in this room, and you will see the angel who will henceforth be your great friend."

Valerianus listened carefully to Cecilia's instructions, and then replied, "As soon as it is daylight, I will do all you have told me, Cecilia. A peaceful joy has taken possession of me, since I promised to believe, and I feel sure it foretells great happiness unknown to me before. And so I leave you, now, to your rest, and may the great God of the Christians guard over you."

He turned and left the room, and Cecilia sank to her knees, murmuring a joyous prayer of thanksgiving to the Virgin, Queen of Heaven.

In this way did Valerianus come to know and believe in the true faith. Early the next morning he set out on the Appian Way and found all as Cecilia had predicted. Urban, upon hearing his story, praised God for His great goodness, and immediately began to instruct the young man in the Holy Scriptures and the main truths of the Christian faith. The beauty and truth of the doctrines captivated Valerianus from the first, and late that afternoon, strong in his belief, he was baptized by Urban in the name of the Father, of the Son, and of the Holy Ghost.

It was with a light and joyous step that he returned toward sunset along the Appian Way to the city. Without delay, he went straight to the room where he knew Cecilia would be waiting for him. He paused before the threshold, overcome with awe and expectancy. Then noiselessly he pushed open the door and stepped into the room. At the far end, her back to him, knelt Cecilia in prayer. Beside her stood a tall, handsome youth, clothed in purest white and shining with an unearthly splendor. Valerianus looked for but a moment, and then withdrew without a sound. Through the deepening dusk he made for the rose garden, there to be alone with his thoughts, and to converse with the God of the Christians, his God now, who had sent down this angel to guard over Cecilia, his virgin wife.

The next few weeks were happy ones for the newly married couple. He, true to his promise, guarded over her as did the angel he had seen. His love for her, immaculate and pure, grew day by day, much in the manner St. Joseph's love must have grown for Mary. Cecilia instructed him more thoroughly in his faith, and Valerianus thought his cup of happiness was full to overflowing when through her, his brother Tiburtius, who had been his inseparable companion from childhood, was also converted. After that, the three made frequent excursions to the poor, assisting and cheering them. The brothers learned the joy there is in helping others, at the cost of self-sacrifice. At night time, too, they sought out the sacred bodies of the martyrs with Cecilia, and reverently bore them to the catacombs for entombment. It was this act of homage to the dead that finally gave all three the crown of martyrdom.

One evening when Valerianus and Tiburtius were gathering up the relics of a martyr, they were seized by the Roman guard and led before Turgius Almachius, the Prefect of the city, who had forbidden anyone to bury the Christians he had put to death.

"Did you not know," he questioned them, "that it is unlawful to bury these Christians?"

"Yes, sir, we did know," replied Valerianus.

"Then truly it is a shame that you two, young Romans of the noblest blood, should so debase yourselves as to break the law, merely because of some religious whim."

"It is not a religious whim, sir," broke in Tiburtius.

"Is it true that you are Christians?" pursued the Prefect.

"Would that we were truly worthy to be called Christians," answered Valerianus humbly.

In the conversation that followed concerning the value of the Christian religion, young Tiburtius grew passionate in his defense of the faith and in his contempt for the Prefect. Finally he cried out:

"How can you, a beast, know aught of what is spiritual?"

The Prefect, instead of being angered by the insult, merely laughed at the fiery spirit of the youth, and had him taken away. Then he turned to question Valerianus, who was more mature and less passionate than his younger brother.

"Young man, how is it that you could embrace such a religion? It deprives you of all the pleasures of this earth. It inflicts pain and suffering upon you. Whereas, if you are true to the religion of your ancestors, yours will be a life full of happiness."

"Did you ever hear the story, sir, of the wise and foolish farmers?" asked Valerianus.

"No, I do not believe I have."

"Then I will tell it to you. Once upon a time, in the spring of the year, certain farmers were laboring hard, ploughing and sowing their fields in the heat of the day. Certain others came by and, seeing them, laughed at their folly in working so hard in the burning sun, while they themselves were going off to drink wine and lie upon the soft grass in the shade.

And so it went on, till the next fall, and those who had labored hard were gathering the harvest into their barns. Now it was their turn to rejoice in the abundance they had stored up for the long winter, while the others who had played away the time of labor, now grieved in their want and suffering. So, too, do the Christians labor and toil now, that for eternity they may rejoice in the abundance of their harvest. And they care not for the jests of idolaters."

"Ah, but we too make provision for the future," replied the Prefect. "We sacrifice to the gods."

"You sacrifice to iron and plaster and demons, we to the one true, living God," answered Valerianus.

At this the Prefect was angered, and much to the joy of Valerianus, had him taken out and scourged for his insolence and blasphemy. During the scourging, a certain Tarquinius stepped up to the Prefect and in secret advised him to put the young men to death, now that there was sufficient evidence against them, because they possessed great wealth which the Prefect might confiscate. The cruel Prefect was grateful for this bit of information and immediately gave the order that the two young men must either offer incense to Jupiter, or be put to death by the sword.

Cecilia in the meantime gained permission to see Valerianus and Tiburtius. She came to them in prison, and they were overjoyed to see her. Not her words alone, but her very presence with them, cheered and comforted them. She repeated to them what they knew well already: that it was a glorious thing and the highest proof of their love to give up their lives for Christ who had died for them. At their parting, they prayed together, and spoke of the joys of the blessed in heaven, which they felt would soon be Cecilia's as well as their own, because she had furnished evidence against herself in coming to them. The two brothers stood side by side and watched her as she left them, Valerianus still weak and pale from the scourging. She glanced around once only, just before she turned out of sight. They knew that, naturally speaking, it must be hard for her to see them condemned to die, but they knew also of her bravery, and of the power her prayers had before the throne of God. In this thought they found strength for the coming ordeal.

The next morning the two were led before a statue of the pagan god, and refusing to offer incense to it, they were led out for execution. Their executioner, Maximus, wept at the sight of such noble youths condemned to die, but they spoke cheerfully to him, and told him of the eternal life in heaven and of the Christian doctrines. Touched by the grace of God, Maximus was converted on the spot. The Prefect was in a rage when he heard of it. He immediately sent a second executioner who beheaded all three of them, and together they entered the courts of heaven, to begin an eternity of happiness.

Cecilia had spent the morning in prayer for Valerianus and Tiburtius. That night after dark, she set out through the narrow streets to find their bodies and that of Maximus. She soon came upon them and with the help of some other Christians, she tenderly, but tearlessly, laid them away in the catacombs. She knew well the tactics of the greedy Prefect, so on the next day, she disposed of all the wealth and property that belonged to Valerianus and herself. She gave most of it to the poor, but through a certain nobleman, a Christian called Gordianus, she left plans for her own house to be converted into a church after her death. Never for a moment did she doubt that she would soon join her husband and brother-in-law in heaven.

By this time the Prefect knew that she was a Christian. He was greatly angered when he found that she had frustrated his plans to get possession of the wealth of Valerianus, and immediately sent for her. He expected to find her a weak young girl whom he could easily win over either by threats or promises. But he was soon disillusioned. From the very first, Cecilia showed herself both quick witted and fearless. Again and again, much to his annoyance, she turned his words back against himself. Nor was she the slightest bit afraid to confess herself a Christian. Finally, after a long discussion ending in failure for the Prefect, he determined to settle the matter.

"I give you one more chance," he told her. "You may offer incense to Jupiter or deny that you are a Christian, and I will pardon you. But if you do neither, I must put you to death."

Cecilia smiled at this. Could he not see how much she desired to die for Christ?

"I am innocent of all crime," she said, "save what you call a crime, that I am a Christian. But call in the accusers you spoke of. Their accusation is my desire, and my punishment is your victory. Thus will we both be satisfied."

"Whence comes such pride?" asked the Prefect.

"It is not pride, but confidence," replied Cecilia. "It is the confidence that comes from a conscience that is unstained."

"But you know," reiterated the Prefect, "that I have power of life and death, granted me by the Emperor."

"It is not true," answered Cecilia. "You have only the power of death: for you can inflict death upon the living, but you cannot give life to the dead."

"A clever play upon words," said the Prefect, "but by the immortal gods, it shall not save you." He realized now what a difficult and futile task he had taken upon himself in trying to dissuade this apparently helpless young woman from her foolish beliefs. Ashamed of his failure and angered by her refutation of his words, he ordered that she be taken to her own home and suffocated in the bath.

Cecilia rejoiced at the order and began immediately to prepare herself for death. They led her to her home and placed her in the bronze bath. Then a huge flame was kept burning under it for a day and a night. Cecilia remained as if in a cool place, untouched by the stifling heat, and praising the goodness and power of God. Again frustrated by this young woman and her religion, the Prefect angrily ordered her to be beheaded there on the very spot where she was. The unskilled executioner struck her three times with his sword, as she knelt with bowed head in prayer, but he was unable to sever the head from the body. Inhumanly, he left her there, half living and half dead. Her friends lifted her up gently and laid her on a couch, where for three days she still lingered on, suffering much, but complaining not at all. By her words, she did not cease to console and strengthen those around her, many of whom she herself had brought into the true fold.

Finally, at the end of the third day, in the presence of Pope Urban and her friends, she ceased speaking to them and began to pray steadily but peacefully. While these prayers were still on her lips, she gave up her precious soul into the hands of the living God, whence it had first come for its short pilgrimage on earth. Urban and the deacons took up her sacred body by night, and laid it away in the catacombs near to the last resting place of Valerianus and Tiburtius.

This, then, is the way in which two noble youths and one noble maiden, beautiful and pure, came home at last to God.

The Flame of Lucca

GEMMA GALGANI

IT WAS getting late, but no one made a move to prepare supper. What was there to prepare? Even the long loaves of bread one could buy so cheaply had become too dear for the Galgani family. But sorrow prevents one from being hungry, and only this morning these sad-faced brothers and sisters had accompanied the rough wooden casket of their father to the cemetery, there to bury him among the poor. Proud Lucca looking on shook her head knowingly, and, like an old wife, whispered a tale about a man who helped others at his own expense and that of his family.

Enrico Galgani had been a prosperous chemist. But because his heart was too big, and because he was too ready to trust everyone who asked for credit, his business gradually grew more and more unsteady. At last, because of bills coming due which he could not meet, all his property was seized, and he and his family were reduced to complete destitution.

Gemma, as long as she lived, would never forget those crushing hours after the funeral, hours that followed one another with the unreal slowness of time in a nightmare. Now in the blue mist of evenfall she looked at the strained pale faces of those about her. What would tomorrow hold for them? In a corner of the room, with eyes smoldering resentment and hands that clenched spasmodically, brooded her eldest brother. It had been hard for him to stand by and watch his father's creditors on the very day of the burial seize what little furniture they had left. One of the scoundrels had even gone to Gemma's purse and taken two lira he found there.

What a difference a few years can make! Gemma's mind went back to those beautiful days when their mother was still alive. It was at her knee that she had first learned to love Jesus. Surely her mother — Gemma brightened at the thought — was a saint in Heaven watching over them. She closed her eyes and prayed to Jesus and her mother.

The poor family had a hard struggle making ends meet until relatives at last came to their assistance. A wealthy aunt of Gemma, attracted by her niece's fascinating smile and beautiful eyes, asked her to come and live with her. Since it meant one less mouth to feed, Gemma was prevailed upon by her brothers to yield.

Every afternoon Gemma and her aunt, both fashionably dressed, would either receive the social elite of Camaiore or repay calls. Much to her aunt's satisfaction, Gemma was becoming the focal point of a great deal of attention. Then one day the blow fell.

The two women were jogging along in their trim open carriage enjoying the pleasant summer lanes, when Gemma felt her aunt's hand press gently upon her own. In response to the girl's questioning smile, her aunt whispered: "Dear, I have a surprise for you. Can you guess?"

Gemma looked mystified.

"It's Giorgio. He has asked to marry you. Gemma, I cannot tell you how happy I am. His is one of the finest families in Italy. And to think that you have captured his heart!"

Gemma was silent, her features immobile and her eyes downcast. She withdrew her hand from her aunt's.

"Are you not pleased?" asked the older woman, a slight flush coming to her cheeks.

"Giorgio is a dear friend," answered Gemma in a low voice, "but I am in love with Someone even more handsome than he."

"Might I ask this gentleman's name?" Gemma could almost feel her aunt's lifted eyebrows as she put this question. Gulping, she replied:

"For a long time my deepest thoughts and affections have been Christ's alone."

"Well, my dear child, for a moment you really frightened me," breathed her aunt in relief. "I thought I had arranged this brilliant match in vain, but I see you are simply under a delusion. You can still love Christ as much as ever. That is a spiritual love; but, my dear, you can also have a natural love for Giorgio which will in no way conflict with it. Many holy women, like Bridget of Sweden, have married, so why not you?" Having finished, she gave Gemma a happy little hug and started planning for the wedding.

It is the biographer's privilege to act the part of a chorus and interpret what is going on in the minds of his characters. At this moment an icy chill comes creeping into Gemma's heart and she is thinking how she can get back to Lucca where she can love Christ alone, even though in poverty and want. From now on the story of Gemma will be the story of her divine romance.

Back home, Gemma was taken with an illness that resulted in curvature of the spine and complete deafness. She suffered the most excruciating tortures for almost a year. An added distress was the burden she believed herself to be upon her impoverished family. But Jesus wished all this suffering for the sanctification of His beloved.

It happened one day after Holy Communion while in the embrace of Jesus. He told her that He wanted her all for Himself and that He, in turn, would be all to her. She understood, then, why He had taken away her mother and father. It was that He might be the sole center of her love. Her sufferings, too, were sent only that she might be one with Him on the Cross.

On June 8, 1899, the vigil of the Feast of the Sacred Heart, Jesus spoke to her: "Courage, Gemma! I await you on Calvary, on the Mount that I shall show you!"

Gemma tells us that in rapture she found herself in the presence of Mary and her Guardian Angel. At the latter's command, she made an act of contrition. Then Mary in the name of her Son forgave her her sins and said: "I will be a mother to you; will you show yourself a true daughter?" Mary then covered Gemma with her mantle. At this moment Jesus appeared and from His sacred wounds darted flames which pierced Gemma's hands and feet and heart. She says she would surely have died had not Mary sustained her. When the vision vanished, Gemma found blood still flowing from the wounds.

This phenomenon was to occur every week on the same day and hour. It began Thursday evening at eight o'clock and lasted till three o'clock on Friday afternoon.

She, who bore the marks of Christ Crucified, was also to lead the life of the Cross. Again and again she was doubted by her relatives, friends, and even her confessor. It seemed as though her Divine Spouse wished Gemma to know thoroughly the terrible loneliness, abandonment, and suspicion He experienced on the Cross.

Extremely sensitive, Gemma was forced to bear the jests of a younger brother who would bring his friends home and command her to go into an ecstasy for their amusement. She had to endure the examination of doctors, though it went against every fiber in her being. Above all this, in moments of severest pain and greatest physical weakness, she had to battle for her very soul.

When someone loves our Lord with a love as tremendous and as pure as Gemma's, you may be sure that the Devil is not going to sit back idle. He is going to do all in his power to destroy and kill it. He is going to direct against it all his craft and cunning.

On several occasions letters were intercepted between Gemma's spiritual father and his Father Provincial, and false ones substituted which claimed that Gemma was a fake and a hypocrite.

Finally, having exhausted all his usual tricks, the Prince of Darkness came in person to attack Gemma. He caused her the most agonizing physical torment so that she was hardly able to pray. He even tried to kill her, and would have done so if Jesus had not prevented him.

He assumed the most horrible shapes. Sometimes he would appear to her as a ferocious dog that would jump upon her breast, or as a giant monster who would beat her all night long while crying: "You belong to me! You belong to me!"

While Gemma was writing a letter to her spiritual father, the Devil would snatch away the pen, tear up the paper, and drag her away from the table. Worst of all, he would try to make her believe that Jesus was cruel for making her suffer so much, or, again, that she was damned.

But through all this, Gemma did not weaken. She had Christ in her heart, and with Him she was unafraid.

In speaking of mystical love, one must always proceed falteringly. How very little, after all, we know of those moments spent on Tabor's heights when the soul and its Beloved merge, as it were, into a single flame.

I record here Gemma's own words as taken down during her ecstasies. They give, I believe, the best description of her consuming love:

Help me, my Strength. Fire! there is fire in my heart this morning; I burn. May I be able day and night to think only of Your glory and love You. I need You, I want You to cleanse me from every stain. Sanctify me, Jesus. Let Your sweetness hold me fast forever. Make me leave earthly things for heavenly, visible things for invisible.

O my God, my Jesus! . . . Jesus, what do You say? O, true Love, You are my God, to You I always turn, to You I am always drawn, to You I want to be united. . . . May the Faith in my heart enlighten my path. Make me know You, O God, that knowing You I know the Truth, Eternity. . . . Who, O God, is like to You? You are omnipotent. My Jesus, true Love, You are my God.

I burn, Jesus. What consolation these flames of Love. . . . Jesus, I have sought Your forgiveness, but this sweetness I have never expected, never merited. . . . I am Yours, do not fear, Jesus, that anyone shall take me from You. Make me love You ever more and more. Jesus, I feel I must die when my heart throbs so.[1]

Gemma's suffering before she died was extreme. Her body agonized in every possible way. The Devil tortured her relentlessly. She begged for her confessor to come and exorcise her that she might have some relief, but this was not to be. All the desolation of Calvary was hers. The last words she uttered were: "Jesus, I commend my poor soul to You."

Gemma died at one o'clock on Holy Saturday, April 11, 1903. Her twenty-five years on earth were lived close to her Crucified Christ. What must have been the joy on that Easter Day when they celebrated their triumph together!

Thirty years later Pope Pius XI proclaimed the little mystic of Lucca, Blessed Gemma Galgani. She was canonized on May 2, 1940, by Pope Pius XII.

[1] Benedict Williamson, *Gemma of Lucca* (St. Louis: Herder Book Co., 1932), pp. 169, 170, 171.

5

The Maid of Orleans
JOAN OF ARC

IT WAS not going to be easy to persuade that gruff old soldier, Robert de Baudricourt, to equip her, a mere girl of sixteen, with arms and men and send her to the king of France with an offer of saving his realm. And she was afraid.

She loved peaceful Domremy, with its simple church, its flocks, its wonderful May tree around which the children danced and sang. Joan was not anxious to give this all up for war and bloodshed. Moreover, it would mean leaving her mother, and her best friends, Mengette and Hauviette. It would mean, likewise, facing the hardships of a soldier's life.

But St. Margaret, St. Catherine, and St. Michael had appeared to her. They had told her that God Himself wished that she should save France. And so again and again she went to see Baudricourt who could further her purpose. But he would not tolerate her until she gave evidence of her mission by telling him of the recent French losses at Rouvray and Orleans, before any messenger could possibly have come from the scene of the conflict. When some days later her statement was confirmed, the hardy old governor of Vaucouleurs was at last won over. He gave her an escort of seven men, and sent her off to the king with the words, "Go, whatever comes of it."

The French court during those days of war and defeat continued its royal gatherings as if the country were enjoying the utmost prosperity. When Joan arrived, the brilliantly lighted hall was alive with smartly uniformed courtiers and women elaborately coiffured and beautifully gowned. They jested about the Maid of Orleans, and thought it rather a lark to receive a farm girl at court. They were not prepared, however, for the little figure clad in black doublet and gray tunic, who walked with such assurance.

As far as she was concerned, the spectacle was not a dazzling one. Had she not spoken with Michael, a courtier of heaven? Were not St. Catherine and St. Margaret her friends? She advanced, appearing to see or hear no one. A false king sat upon the throne, placed there to test the statements she made that saints and angels guided her in her actions. She ignored him, and going straight to Charles, the true king, she knelt before him.

"God give you long life, noble king."

But Charles answered, "I am not the king."

"In God's Name, Sir, you are the king, and no other." The firmness with which Joan spoke, caused the king to marvel at the little peasant girl. "Give me troops wherewith to succor Orleans and to guard you to Rheims to be anointed and crowned. For it is the Will of God."

Then Charles talked to her privately for a time, and in this talk she gave him the Sign by which he might know the genuineness of his mission. Some say she told him of a prayer he had once made to know whether he was the true king or no, a prayer which he told to no man, and which she assured him had been answered by God. Then did the king believe in her.

However, ordinary prudence demanded that trial must be made of her claims, and the University of Poitiers was chosen to conduct the trial. Joan submitted, and thrilled the court with the defense she made of herself and her claims. The learned doctors who were her judges were fully convinced that she was sent by God, and advised the king not to reject her. The trial was duly recorded, but a little more than a year later, when Joan was captured by the English and tried for witchcraft, these records, which she needed so, were nowhere to be found. Were they destroyed? Treacherously? Joan was wont to say that the only enemy she feared was treachery. Poor girl, she was to meet plenty of it.

Six weeks were consumed by this trial, but the king was convinced of her mission, and was ready at last to use her for France. A suit of white armor was made for her at Tours, and a charger given her, all from the king. Her standard was patterned after the direction of the Voices — the voices of Catherine, Margaret, and Michael that spoke to her and bade her what to do. Joan refused the sword offered her by the king, intending to slay no one in battle. But some sort of sword a soldier must have, and her Voices told her where to find one. At the shrine of St. Catherine of Fierbois, behind the altar, was an old sword buried in the ground. This should be hers. So they dug there as Joan commanded, and found it to their great surprise, and sent it to her, all burnished.

Her most faithful captains from now to the end were the Duke D'Alençon of the blood royal, Jean D'Aulnon, her faithful squire, and the fiery warrior La Hire, who with his band of "hellions," as he called them, were willing to follow her anywhere and everywhere. When Joan first took charge

diate action. Policy and diplomacy she declared would result only in harmful delay.

"Pray tell then," someone asked her, "how would you go about treating with the English?"

"At the point of the lance!" she cried, with eyes afire.

The king was finally persuaded and gave her leave to act, and immediately towns and forts began to fall to her in quick succession. First Jargeau, then Meung and Beaugency. Finally she won the great victory at Patay, defeating that formidable English soldier, Talbot. This was the first French victory in the open field. Now was Charles willing to march to Rheims.

It was a glorious affair, the coronation. Right into the crowded cathedral, still mounted, the king entered, and his company with him. Then four of the chief military officers, also mounted, rode in, bearing the sacred *ampoule* or cruet of oil, with which all the kings of France were anointed. Next to the king stood Joan with her standard, radiant with joy, and all about were bishops and nobles. When the king was finally anointed and the archbishop had set the crown on his head, the thunderous cheers almost rent the roof of the cathedral. And Joan, in a flood of hot tears, knelt and embraced the knees of the king and kissed his foot.

"Now, gentle king," she said, "is the will of God accomplished, who wished you to be crowned as the lawful king of the realm of France."

She now asked to be allowed to return to Domremy. Joan had enough of war, but Charles would not have her go. So Joan stayed, but her Voices, though they spoke to her, and appeared to her still, no longer advised her in matters of war. Now it is that Joan's life becomes a tragic one. From now to the end she meets with nothing but treachery.

For a year she was allowed to carry on occasional unimportant skirmishes, and then came the awful news! Joan was captured by the Burgundians and imprisoned in the tower of Beaurevoir.

She was so frightened at the English, for they made all sorts of threats against her, that she determined to escape from the tower which was her prison. St. Catherine forbade her to escape, but she nevertheless, tied strips of cloth together, and letting herself out the window, began to descend when her makeshift rope broke, and she fell to the ground. No bones were broken, but she was found unconscious, and for several days could neither eat nor drink. It was the only time she had disobeyed her Voices, but they told her that her fault was forgiven. When this escape was later adduced against her in her trial at the hands of the English, Joan answered simply:

"It is the right of every prisoner."

Joan was captured in May, and from then to the end of the year she was kept prisoner, and guarded by coarse soldiers who made her life intolerable. They never left her out of their sight, and in dread of them and their vileness she continued to wear her male attire and would not take a woman's.

Then in January an ecclesiastical court was ordered to try the simple and holy Joan of Arc for heresy, witchcraft, and blasphemy, with the infamous Cauchon, Bishop of Beauvais, presiding.

The trial proceeded, with Joan deprived of even the outward forms of justice. They continued to keep her in the dungeon between sessions, chained by the neck, feet, and hands, poorly fed, and exposed to the brutality of the guards. The sessions themselves lasted several hours apiece; no counsel was given her, and she was continually harassed with questions by some seventy learned doctors of theology of the University of Paris. To all of them she responded clearly, often quite wittily, and always wisely. She was asked, for instance, which of the Popes at Rome was the true one. It must be remembered that at this time there were several claimants to the papal throne. Joan answered cleverly, "Are there two?" Another asked her, "Why did you take the horse which belonged to the Bishop of Senlis? Was not that stealing?" Joan answered, "The horse was taken without my approval, and was paid for. Besides, the hackney was useless for campaigns, and was sent back."

At one of the later sessions a certain doctor was to summarize all the facts of the entire trial into one speech, and thus make the case appear black for Joan. He brought his speech with him, committed to a bulky mass of manuscript, but began to deliver it from memory. After a few minutes he paused, consulted his manuscript and went on, only to have his memory fail again. After the third lapse, Joan looked up with an innocent smile and said, *"Read* your book."

Most of the sessions, however, were weary affairs, with constant repetitions of the same themes: her Voices, her sign to the king, the question of male attire, and complete submission to the Church. Joan would answer wearily, "I have answered that before," or "That does not pertain to the trial." And when they became particularly wearisome, she would say, "I will answer no more today," and the court would perforce adjourn.

For five long months they plagued her, but were no nearer to proving their trumped-up charges than they were at the beginning. Finally they held a session outdoors, in front of a stake piled round with fagots, and threatened Joan that if she did not abjure she would be burned. She said she did not know what abjuration was. One of the judges explained to her that if she signed a paper, a short one no longer than eight lines, she would be allowed to be kept in an ecclesiastical prison free of her chains, with women guarding her. The paper said nothing but that Joan confessed and abjured in general any wrong she might have committed, and that she agreed to put away her male attire. She signed, as much through fear of the fire as from a wish to have done with this trial and be freed from her horrible prison. And here took place the cruelest act of deceit in the whole process, for taking advantage of her inability to read, they substituted another paper in place of the one she agreed to sign, in which they made her confess herself guilty of mortal sin, witchcraft, blasphemy, idolatry, and every evil act of which they had accused her before this. And to make her cup of bitterness full, when she asked them to send her now to an ecclesiastical prison, Bishop Cauchon answered, "Take her back whence she came."

They took her back to her prison, and gave her a woman's dress. But during the night they took it away, and put in its place the male attire which she had worn. Having nothing else to wear, Joan was forced to resume man's clothing. This was reported to the authorities who scarce could restrain their joy. A couple of days later in a hurried session, and in Joan's absence, the court condemned her as a heretic, and handed her over to the secular arm for punishment — which was the terrible death by fire at the stake.

On May the thirtieth Joan was informed of the death she was to die that day. She burst into piteous tears and asked, "Will they treat me so horribly? And must my body which has never been violated be burned to ashes? I would prefer to be beheaded seven times than to die so."

A tremendous crowd had gathered to witness the execution; there were people everywhere: in windows, on the branches of trees, even on the roofs of houses. Joan was first preached at by one of the doctors of theology, and then roughly bound to a stake erected on a high platform. She asked for a crucifix, and an English soldier made a cross of a piece of wood and gave it to her. The faggots were then ignited, and for awhile Joan suffered dreadfully as the fire, slow in starting, licked up at her from below. But at last the wood caught well, and a merciful sheet of flame rose up and enveloped her as she cried out loudly: "Jesus!" It was the final act in the tragedy of a lovable maid, the holiest and most courageous character that ever lived for France.

6

The Shepherdess of Our Lady
BERNADETTE

NOTHING ever happened in Lourdes; nothing very remarkable had ever happened there; and no one ever thought that one day the little city would become famous all over the world, and that a million people a year would come to visit it. Tourists seldom, if ever, came to the French village at the foot of the wooded Pyrenees. For one thing, Lourdes was nine miles from the nearest railroad and the mild grandeur of the Pyrenees, running off into the plain, do not have the rugged splendor of the Alps. Then, too, except for the old rock fortress which stood high on a scarped rock in the center of the town and which had seen Roman and Saracen, English and French garrisons, there was little of historical note in Lourdes. St. Dominic had preached in Lourdes, but so had he preached in every other town of southern France. The Huguenot Jeanne d'Albret had cruelly persecuted the people of Lourdes, but persecution was an honor shared by millions in France during the seventeenth century. With such an uneventful history covering well over a thousand years surely nothing of world-wide significance could be expected to come from Lourdes, and least of all from the Soubirous family. But the event which was to happen was truly to be remarkable.

In all the seven valleys which ran together to make the

village there was not a poorer family to be found. François Soubirous was a miller by trade. He had lived with his wife, Louise, and his children in some cold, damp mills, but the family's latest dwelling was the worst. It was a gloomy place, colder and even damper than the mills. A wall about four feet from the house shut out much of the light. There were bars on the two windows and behind one of these a broken pane of glass. A flat stone served for a table and there was one chair and three beds which had to do for the mother, father, and four children. A meaner dwelling could hardly have been found, for the Soubirous were living in the *cachot* (dungeon), the abandoned prison of Lourdes.

To those who are really poor in spirit, poverty has never been a reproach. From the lowly cave of Bethlehem came forth the Leader of God's people, Israel, from the wretched *cachot* of Lourdes came one who was destined to make the name of Lourdes familiar to every Catholic ear.

Bernadette, the eldest child of François and Louise Soubirous, was born in the mill of Boly, January 7, 1844. Two days later she was baptized and given the name Marie-Bernard. Although she was later called by the diminutive "Bernadette," our Blessed Mother never forgot that the child had been dedicated especially to herself.

At the time of Bernadette's birth the family was fairly well off. When her father, François, had married he had taken over the management of the mill of Boly in the Lapaca quarter of Lourdes. What should have furnished a good livelihood to any man of even moderate skill proved a financial loss under the mismanagement of poor François, who for all his good will, was a mediocre craftsman and a very bad collector. As his family increased, so did his debts, until finally in 1855 they were forced to leave the mill as he could no longer pay the rent. In a Puritan community where sanctity so often tends to be measured by financial success, François would certainly have appeared to be a considerable sinner, if not positively damned. He had no better success in the mill of Baudéan, or the mill of Escoubés. The family was soon destitute, and, but for the kindness of a relative who let them use the abandoned prison, they would hardly have had a home in which to live.

The children for lack of food and fuel were often enough forced to go to bed cold and supperless. Jean-Marie, the eldest son, was even seen scraping up the wax drippings of the candles in the church and eating them to satisfy his hunger. Poverty, toil, and sickness go hand in hand, and Bernadette, the eldest, had an abundance of all three. Although she was still a child much of the care of the younger children fell upon her. She washed, scrubbed, and baked and she had no time to go to school. She took it as a matter of course that she was often ill from the asthma which lasted with her to the end of her life. The *cachot* was certainly no Paradise, but God who loves the poor in spirit, must have looked with special delight upon the Soubirous, who for all their misery never ceased to trust in Him. Every night the father, mother, and children could be seen kneeling together to recite the rosary.

Their prayers were in a manner answered, for in 1857 Bernadette went to live with the Aravants in Bartres, a little mountain village some two miles from Lourdes. Marie Aravant had been Bernadette's nurse, and she invited her to come and take care of her children. Her husband, however, was a stingy fellow and Bernadette soon discovered that her work would be that of a shepherdess.

Was life at this time lonely for her? Perhaps not, for this quiet girl with her thoughtful eyes and simple manner had her rosary to say and wild flowers to pick for the shrines which she built of stone for our Blessed Mother. Moreover, she had her lambs to watch. Seated on a stone with Pigou, the dog, watching the sheep, or eating her bit of brown bread, or accepting gratefully some little sweet from one of the neighbors who knew of Aravant's stinginess, one wonders if Bernadette did not have occasion to think of some of those famous shepherds and shepherdesses of history.

Was it not to the shepherd Moses that God had appeared in the Burning Bush commanding him to lead His people out of Egypt? Was it not to the young shepherd David that the command was sent to leave his flocks and his father's house and to lead the armies of Israel? And the deeds of her own countrywoman, Joan of Arc, the shepherdess of Domremy, were they less glorious? Leaving her family and her flocks *la Pucelle,* as the French fondly called her, had led the armies of France to victory, crowned Charles VII at Rheims, and perished in flames, a martyr at the stake. Probably none of these thoughts passed through the mind of Bernadette as morning and evening she led the sheep to the common pastures on the mountain slopes about Bartres. But she at least knew that it was to the shepherds that the good tidings of our Lord's birth were sent, and that He had not hesitated to call Himself "the Good Shepherd."

Toward the end of 1857 another thought painful but sweet haunted Bernadette. She would be fourteen, she knew, in January, and she had not yet made her First Holy Communion. The young shepherdess longed for the time when the priest in Mary's stead would bring Jesus to her heart. So it was, that she returned to Lourdes at the end of January. She would study with the other children in Lourdes in preparation for this great event of her life.

The days passed quietly. There was never too much to eat in the poor *cachot,* never much fuel to drive away the winter chill or dampness from the stone walls. What is more, the wood for the hearth had to be gathered from beneath the trees in the woods overlooking the Gave de Pau and carried home. It was on one of these foraging expeditions in the afternoon of February 11, 1858, that Bernadette, her sister Toinette, and Jeanne Abadie came to the canal of the mill of Savy where it plunged at the base of the cliff Massabielle into the swift-flowing Gave.

Her two companions quickly slipped off their shoes and stockings and splashed across the stream crying out to Bernadette that the water was very cold. Bernadette hesitated. Should she follow? A cold might bring a spell of asthma. Gathering a few loose stones she tried to make steps for herself in the canal. Failing in this, she stooped down to loosen her sabots, those odd leathern shoes with wooden soles which make such a decided clatter on the frozen ground or cobblestone path. But, what was that she heard? It sounded like a strong wind, which was strange for a chill and cloudy afternoon. The girl looked up but could see nothing. All was perfectly still. Again she started to remove her stockings when for a second time she heard the sound.

Bernadette was frightened, she stood up and saw opposite her a bush moving as by a strong wind while all else was still. Then from a cave or natural grotto at the base of the cliff she saw a golden cloud emerge and soon after a beautiful Lady.

The Lady was young, as young and fair as the spring of the year or the two yellow roses which rested so lightly on her sandalless feet. She could not have been more than sixteen or seventeen, and she stood poised on a wild rose bush, in a lancet-shaped cleft in the rock, to the right of the grotto of Massabielle. Her eyes were blue and kindly, and her hair was all but covered by a white veil. Her dress was white — whiter than any bleaching could have made it, and around her waist was a blue ribbon which flowed down along her robe. From her arm hung a rosary of pure white beads strung upon a golden chain.

The Lady smiled at the wondering girl and made a sign for her to come nearer. Startled and afraid Bernadette blinked, then rubbed her eyes but still the Lady was there. Taking out her rosary Bernadette fell on her knees. This seemed to please the Lady for she too counted the prayers on her rosary, and, what is more, she joined Bernadette in saying the "Glory be to the Father. . . ." All fear had left Bernadette, yet when the Lady again beckoned her to approach she dared not go. And then the Lady vanished.

Who was the beautiful Lady? Bernadette was not so sure. Had Jeanne and Toinette seen anything? Why no, what made her ask? When the two girls had promised that they would tell no one Bernadette finally told them what she had seen. But that night, when at their evening prayers Bernadette had begun to cry, her younger sister told her mother what had happened by the rock of Massabielle. Madame Soubirous was alarmed; she told Bernadette to stop her dreaming and above all not to go back to the cliff and the grotto.

But something was calling Bernadette back toward the rock, and it was something which she could not resist. Toinette and Jeanne finally persuaded her mother to let her return. It was three days later, after she had been to Sunday Mass, that she set out for the grotto with five of her young friends. On their way they stopped at the church to get some holy water with which to protect themselves in case the apparition was that of an evil spirit. When they arrived at the rock they knelt to say the rosary.

"She is there! She is smiling!" Bernadette suddenly cried with delight.

Taking the holy water and sprinkling it as she went toward the Lady she said: "If you are from God, stay!" Then she knelt motionless and in an ecstasy.

Her friends began to cry as they saw nothing and were afraid that Bernadette might die. A rock cast from the top of the cliff by some children terrified them as at first they did not know from where it came. Bernadette, however, was not conscious of any of their fears. When she had at length been led away from the spot the vision disappeared. But henceforth, though she still remained the simple peasant girl that she was, Bernadette could not forget the Lady she had seen. Who was she? Bernadette did not know, the Lady had not revealed her name.

The next Thursday, for a third time the vision appeared to Bernadette as she knelt before the grotto. Two ladies who had armed themselves with a blessed candle, and paper, pen, and ink accompanied her. The latter, they thought, would be of use in case the mysterious visitor had some message to impart. When Bernadette offered these to her the Lady smiled and said:

"I need not write what I have to say to you. Will you do me the favor of returning here every day for a fortnight?"

"Yes, indeed!" replied the enchanted girl, "if my parents will let me."

In all, the vision lasted for nearly an hour. Before the Lady disappeared she outlined the whole of Bernadette's life in the few words:

"I do not promise you that you will be happy in this world, but in the next."

Probably the message meant little to Bernadette at the time, for what greater happiness could she conceive than that of seeing the Lady of the grotto during the next two weeks? The next day her mother and her Aunt Bernarde accompanied Bernadette to the grotto. As she saw her child in ecstasy Madame Soubirous must have felt something of that which Mary and Joseph felt as they stood in admiration of the Child Jesus in the temple. Could this child be her daughter? And yet she was afraid. "My God," she was heard to pray, "do not take my child from me!" As for the little band of villagers that had gathered about the rock, when they saw the girl so intent in prayer, they could but whisper to each other, "How beautiful she is!"

Like a fire in a stubble field which at first catches only a few stalks and consumes them, but then, borne by the wind, leaps from row to row till finally a whole vast field has been swept, the news of Bernadette's visions raged throughout the countryside. Never had such a strange story been heard in Lourdes or the surrounding villages. Even the legend of

Charlemagne and the Saracen Mirat on the coat of arms of Lourdes could not compare with this.

"Who was this Bernadette?" "Was she a dreamer, or a mystic, or someone old in sanctity if not in age?" "Was she brilliant or talented or wonderfully fair like Cinderella of the fairy tale?"

No, Bernadette was none of these as those who knew her and those who came to the grotto soon could see. The days of princesses and fairy godmothers were past. Bernadette was plain and simple, unimaginative, and of the poorest of the poor. She was small for her age with smooth dark hair and rather thoughtful eyes. And, though she could neither read nor write, her soul was as pure as the fresh mountain air, or the numerous fountains and streams in the valleys about her native Lourdes.

At the sixth apparition which took place early in the morning of Sunday, February 21, Doctor Dozous, a well-known but skeptical physician, was converted to a belief in the supernatural. To him it was evident that there could be no other explanation for the ecstatic state of Bernadette during the vision. She was not the victim of hallucination for her pulse was normal and her breathing regular and she retained the use of her faculties. There were others, however, who were not so easily convinced.

The commotion about the grotto of Massabielle was too much for the anticlerical officials of the town. They were determined to put a stop to this foolish superstition. Bernadette was brought before the Mayor and questioned. At the end of the investigation he said:

"Will you promise me not to return to Massabielle?"

"No, sir," she replied, "I cannot promise that."

"Is this your final decision?"

"Yes, sir."

"Enough! you may go, we will see what is to be done."

The next to take up the investigation was Monsieur Jacomet, the Chief of Police. Monsieur Jacomet prided himself on being something of a detective. His method was original enough. At Bernadette's dictation he wrote down an account of the apparitions and then read it back to her after he had changed several of the details. His attempts to confuse Bernadette were unsuccessful; at every error he was corrected. This first encounter with the civic authorities seemed to be a complete victory for the peasant girl but they had other means at their disposal.

The preceding spring François Soubirous had spent several days in the city jail on what seems to have been an unsubstantiated charge of stealing bread and wood. The poor are easily victimized, they have few lawyers to defend them. François wished no further clashes with the law. What would his family do if he were again forced into jail? Frightened by the threats of the Chief of Police he promised that Bernadette would never again be permitted to return to the grotto.

To the girl who had been counting each moment to the time when she would again see the beautiful Lady there could have been nothing more severe. She had promised the Lady that she would return but her parents forbade it. The dilemma was complete; it meant that she must either obey her parents or the Lady of the Grotto. She chose the former.

Since her return from Bartres Bernadette had been attending school at the Hospice conducted by the Sisters of Charity of Nevers. The day after her father had forbidden her to return to the grotto, as she was returning to school after her meager noonday meal, she was stopped at a point in the road which leads from the Pont des Ruisseaux to the convent by what seemed an invisible barrier. Try as she might she could not go farther; she was being called to the grotto by the Gave de Pau and she soon found herself kneeling before it. Here a real trial awaited her for the Lady did not appear.

That night when her father noticed her great unhappiness he withdrew his prohibition. She could go to the grotto as often as she pleased. Trials, however great they may be, seldom last for long. Spring comes after winter; and after night the day. The next morning her Lady of the grotto came again.

What did the people think of these strange apparitions? The attitude of the police was plain enough. The clergy were keeping strictly aloof, not wishing to commit themselves on such a delicate question. The newspapers were scoffing at the whole affair. But the rough peasants and hardy mountaineers and the stalwart quarrymen from the slate mines in the mountains firmly believed that Bernadette was really speaking with a saint, perhaps even with the Queen of all saints, the Blessed Virgin. Yet even these men and women who had none of the withering skepticism of the more learned were puzzled and disturbed by the strange actions of Bernadette at the ninth apparition.

It was Thursday, February 25; some five hundred had gathered about the base of the cliff before Bernadette arrived.

She began her prayers and was soon rewarded by the appearance of the Lady. Twice, as if she had been ordered by the Lady, she went within the grotto. After she had returned to her original place she began to walk toward the river as if she were seeking something. Evidently what she was looking for was not there as she turned and retraced her steps to the far end of the grotto. There she knelt and dug a hole in the moist earth with her hand. Soon the little hollow in the ground filled with muddy water. When she had scooped up a bit of this with her cupped hand she drank it. As if this were not enough, with both of her hands she washed her face with the water and then plucked and ate some herbs that were growing close by.

The people began to wonder if the poor girl were not losing her wits. What could she have possibly meant by drinking that muddy water and smearing her face with it? When asked later why she had acted so strangely Bernadette simply replied that the Lady had told her to "Go, drink and wash at the spring." She knew of no spring so she had started for the river. The Lady then pointed to the inside of the grotto and there she had uncovered it.

Soon the flow of water increased in volume and the next day when Bernadette returned it was flowing strongly. The spring still flows today at the rate of a thousand gallons an hour and it has become the most famous spring in all the world. Of course, this was all unknown at the time of its discovery and there must have been many a one who asked himself what in the world the spring was good for. And the water which Bernadette discovered was not even mineral water. Its chemical constituents were just the same as that of countless other springs in southern France. The skeptics

would probably have been satisfied if Bernadette had uncovered a pot of gold or a vein of silver, or some inland oyster
concealing a lustered pearl within its slimy folds. Certainly
the family could have used any one of these. But water!
Water turning the wheels of her father's mill had brought
neither luck nor fortune. And if there was anything which
the people of Lourdes did not need it was water. The Gave
de Pau with its tumbling, flashing waters slipped past the
town. The mills all had their canals, and the valleys about
Lourdes all had their little springs which were fed by the
shimmering snow of the Pyrenees.

The evening of the day on which she had discovered the
spring Bernadette with her Aunt Basile went to visit the
Abbé Peyramale, the parish priest of Lourdes. The Abbé
was a rugged mountaineer with iron gray hair, sharp features,
and eyebrows like the proverbial storm clouds. The priest
was gruff, he wanted to make no mistake! He had already
heard of the strange antics of the morning.

"You've been eating grass like the animals," was his not
too favorable comment on the morning's proceedings. His
final words were, "Leave me in peace, or I shall chase you
with a broom; you have seen nothing."

No doubt Bernadette would have gladly left the good
Curé at peace, but the Lady would not let her. Two days
later, on Saturday, February 27, she ordered Bernadette:

"Go tell the priests that a chapel should be built here."

On March 2 she had another message for them:

"I desire to see processions made to this spot."

M. Peyramale was taken aback by the requests. He could
not doubt Bernadette's sincerity yet she might be the victim

of some delusion. Then, too, why had the Lady not revealed her name?

The crowds which had gathered about the grotto of Massabielle to see Bernadette in ecstasy steadily increased. At first only a handful were present, then two hundred, five hundred, eight hundred, and later two thousand. On March 3 some four thousand had assembled and on the following day, the last day of the fortnight, over twenty thousand were present. There were newspapermen from Paris, shepherds from the neighborhood of Tarbes and Bartres, and housewives from Lourdes and the neighboring valleys. They came on foot, on horseback, or riding in jolting two-wheeled carts. Some, like Zacheus of old, climbed up into the trees or the rocks overhanging the grotto for a better view. Thousands of others were crowded together on the opposite bank of the river. Even the Mayor and the Chief of Police were there, and the troops had been called out to maintain order. Through this dense and excited throng two gendarmes with drawn swords led Bernadette, all unconscious of the crowd and only intent on again seeing her well-beloved Lady.

In a way the people were disappointed; for nothing occurred by the grotto except Bernadette's usual ecstasy which so many of them had already witnessed. The Lady had not revealed herself to them as they had hoped; she had not even told her name. She had come, she had disappeared without saying farewell; neither Bernadette nor the people of Lourdes could believe that the Lady had gone from their beautiful land forever.

It was the eve of the Annunciation, three weeks later, that Bernadette felt to her great joy that she was being again

called to the grotto. Early the next morning she set forth.
She was not to be alone, for already a good crowd of fervent
souls who expected that the Lady would surely have something to say on this great feast, had gathered by the rock.
When she arrived, Bernadette found that the Lady was there
waiting for her. Her first thought was to ask the Lady's
pardon for coming late. The answer was reassuring and
Bernadette entered into an ecstasy which lasted nearly an
hour. Who was the Lady? This time Bernadette did not forget to ask her name. Taking courage from the graciousness
of her visitor she asked three times: "Madame, [my Lady]
would you be so kind as to tell me who you are?" At the
third earnest plea the Lady joined her hands, looked up to
heaven, and then, leaning forward toward the anxious girl
replied:

"*Que soy era Immaculado Counceptiou!*"

"I am the Immaculate Conception!"

The message, which had been delivered in the humble
patois of the Pyrenees, a mixture of French and Spanish,
Bernadette kept repeating to herself as she hurried toward
the parish house to inform the Abbé Peyramale. She had not,
as she later admitted, the slightest idea what the words could
mean. But the Curé and the whole town of Lourdes at once
caught their significance. Less than four years before, on
December 8, 1854, Pius IX had solemnly defined the dogma
of the Immaculate Conception of the Blessed Virgin Mary.
Was it any wonder then that a wave of enthusiasm swept the
town? For had not the Mother of God appeared in their land
and shown how well she had been pleased by this decree?

On two more occasions did Mary, the Immaculate Conception, appear to Bernadette. On April 7, as she knelt in

ecstasy before the rock, Doctor Dozous who happened to be present saw her left hand pass over the flame of a candle which she held in her right hand. Since the flame seemed to do her no harm he forbade the bystanders to extinguish it. For a full quarter of an hour Bernadette's hand was over the flame. Not only did she feel no pain but the hand showed no signs of injury. After the ecstasy Doctor Dozous passed the candle under her hand several times but each time Bernadette withdrew it quickly with the words:

"You are burning me!"

The first apparition of our Blessed Mother to Bernadette took place on February 11, the Feast of St. Genevieve, the patroness of shepherds. On the Feast of the Annunciation, when on every side the trees were bursting forth like stars in the growing twilight, reminding mankind of the coming of our Lord to a sin-sodden world, Mary announced that she was the Immaculate Conception. And it was on July 16, the Feast of Our Lady of Mount Carmel, that she appeared to Bernadette for the last time here on earth. In the meantime, on the Feast of Corpus Christi, June 3, Bernadette had made her First Holy Communion, and it was on the day on which she had received our Lord for the third time that Mary appeared to her. The authorities, still obstinate in their persecution, had boarded up the entrance to the grotto, and so Bernadette was forced to kneel on the other side of the Gave de Pau. But as she later wrote: "I saw neither the Gave nor the barrier. The distance between the Lady and me appeared no greater than usual. I saw nothing but the Blessed Virgin, and never had I seen her so beautiful."

Although she was never again to have the happiness of

seeing the Mother of God upon earth Bernadette still had a mission to perform. The Lady had asked for a chapel to be built and processions to come to the spring. The petty persecution of the town officials was stopped by a telegram from Napoleon III, but the authorities of the Church were slow in giving their official approval. The Abbé Peyramale, once converted, proved a stanch ally and defender of Bernadette. He strongly supported a commission which was formed in July by the Bishop of Tarbes to make an ecclesiastical investigation. The inquiry was extremely thorough, and it was not until four years later, on January 18, 1862, that a pastoral letter was sent to the clergy and faithful of the diocese giving approval to the devotion which had rapidly grown up at Lourdes. In his approbation the Bishop stated:

It is our verdict that the Immaculate Mary, Mother of God, did really appear to Bernadette Soubirous, on February 11, 1858, and on subsequent days, eighteen times in all, at the Grotto of Massabielle, near to the town of Lourdes.

To many of the pilgrims who came to the grotto in those first few years Bernadette was not less an attraction than the spring. The *cachot* was constantly besieged by people of wealth or influence who wished to see this favorite child of Mary. Many of these seeing the dire poverty of the Soubirous tried, with as much tact as they could muster, to give the family some little support. But they were all refused. Often someone would leave a coin on the table or window sill and the coin was as often promptly returned. The *cachot* had become well known, in fact, to the Bishop's mind, it was getting far too much publicity. Poverty was admirable, but destitution was something else. With his aid the Soubirous were able to move in January, 1859, to a little mill.

In July, 1860, Bernadette was received into the Hospice of Lourdes. In this combination school and hospital she had prepared for her First Holy Communion and had received the little schooling which she possessed. Ill health from lack of nourishment and asthma, and the frequent visitors who came to see her made the change advisable. Besides, she could more easily continue her lessons with the other pupils of the Sisters of Charity.

During the first few months of her stay at the Hospice Bernadette nearly died from an inflammation of the lungs, and the visitors came as frequently as ever. Distasteful as the frequent summons to the parlor must have been Bernadette never failed to narrate the story of the apparitions. If the incredulous would not believe she would not argue: "I tell you what I saw and what I heard," she would say; "if you do not choose to believe me, what more can I do?" Her position was, to say the least, unique, and many an embarrassing situation Bernadette was able to save with her native sense of humor. To one perfervid woman who had knelt for her blessing she said: "You see that I have no stole! Wait at least until the bishop has given me his powers." So much attention and adulation might have turned the head of one who was less humble than Bernadette. In her own opinion she was nothing but a poor peasant girl whom our Lady had chosen as her instrument, "a broom to be used and then laid away in a corner." She would have been the last of all to consider herself a saint.

After the approbation of the Bishop the work toward the construction of a suitable chapel for our Lady advanced. In 1864 a marble statue was placed at the grotto; and two years later, on May 21, 1866, the crypt of the projected church which had been built into the rock of Massabielle was declared open to the public. Our Lady had asked for a chapel and they were building her a magnificent basilica. Bernadette's task was near completion.

There have been great heroes of God who have gone forth from the quiet of a university, or cloistered retreat "to set the world on Fire," as St. Francis Xavier was sent by St. Ignatius. Others have always stood in the public eye, such as St. Louis of France. Still more have spurned all the honors that the world showered on them and have hidden themselves in the obscurity of a religious house. As Bernadette saw the task to which she had been committed becoming more and more of a realization, it was but natural that she should think of her vocation in afterlife. For some time she had thought of entering a convent, but she believed herself unworthy of that great privilege. To the Bishop of Nevers, who had come to see her, she expressed her desires and her doubts:

"I am poor and without aptitude for any particular work, so I can hardly hope to be received into the convent."

Needless to say, her own estimation was not that of others. She was accepted at the Convent of St. Gildard, the Mother House of the Sisters of Charity and Christian Instruction of Nevers.

Although she had been accepted as a candidate, Bernadette was detained two more years at Lourdes by her ill health. Finally the day of parting, which had been set for July 4, 1866, was at hand. On the evening of her departure Bernadette paid a last visit to the Rock of Massabielle and the Grotto which she loved so well. She knew that she would never again see the spring which Mary had so kindly pointed out to her. As great as is the joy of meeting so must be the sadness of parting in this life. A fervent prayer, a kiss and tear that fell upon the rock — these must have lasted long in the memory of Bernadette. To a Sister whom she had known at Lourdes she wrote from the Convent of St. Gildard:

"Pray for me when you go to the Grotto; it is there that you will find me, cleaving to the rock which I love so dearly."

A holy man once wrote that God has hidden the joys of the religious life from the people of the world or else all men would be in monasteries; and another, that no one can here long abide unless he be willing to humble himself with all his heart for the love of God. The two but mean that one must come to realize what even pagans have understood: there is nothing nobler than suffering with a high motive for a great purpose. If to bear the cross bravely is the lot of every Christian, much more is it the lot of one who is destined to become a saint. Bernadette with the greatest patience and cheerfulness bore sufferings that few are asked to bear. Her Superiors, fearing that the constant visitors and the extraordinary favors which she had received might make her proud, continually reproved and humbled her. Sickness was her constant companion. While at Lourdes pilgrims by the hundreds were being cured, she received no help from the violent attacks of asthma to which she had been subject from childhood. To this was added the excruciating pain of an abscess and tumor which formed upon her knee.

In the convent Bernadette fulfilled the tasks of infirmarian and sacristan, but the most difficult task of all was that of patient suffering. On the afternoon of April 16, 1879, she died with a final prayer to her Lady of the Grotto:

"Holy Mary, Mother of God, pray for me, a poor sinner . . . a poor sinner . . ."

If the body of Bernadette was found incorrupt twenty years after her death, and if numerous miracles have been attributed to her intercession, we may be sure that her life of obscurity was not wasted. The cause of her beatification was introduced and after the regular processes she was beatified by Pius XI on June 14, 1925. Eight years later she was canonized on a day which had been a favorite of hers, December 8, 1933, the Feast of the Immaculate Conception.

Perhaps a final word should be said about the land which the simple shepherdess made famous. Lourdes is still today a land of prodigies. Here the blind see, the lame walk, the deaf hear, and the poor not only have the gospel preached to them but they are cared for by members of the noblest families of France. Here to the left of the grotto one can see hundreds of crutches which have been left by people who have been cured at Lourdes. Here in a thousand ways the laws of medicine are flouted. To the shrine of our Lady of Lourdes the sick and dying are brought from all parts of the world and no one is the worse for the experience. The sick at their own request are plunged into the icy waters of the spring. No one has ever suffered ill effects from the rigorous treatment, while hundreds have been cured. In the first fifty years of the shrine's existence three thousand nine hundred and sixty-two partial or complete cures were recorded at the medical bureau of the shrine and these were perhaps only half of the cures which took place. Here where the dogma of the Immaculate Conception was so strikingly confirmed another proclamation of the church has been confirmed. Since 1905, when Pius X advocated the practice of frequent Communion, more miracles have been wrought during the procession of the Blessed Sacrament at Lourdes than in the baths themselves.

Little wonder is it, then, that Lourdes has become the most famous shrine of Mary in the world, and that people from China and Japan, England and Peru, from India and the United States have made it the object of their pilgrimage. Many books have been written about Lourdes and Bernadette by Catholics, Protestants, and atheists. Rationalists such as Huxley and Emile Zola have gone so far as to deny and distort the evident facts. But the facts remain — who can believe that the instantaneous cure of cancer, and lupus, and fractured bones is a natural thing? The rock of Massabielle from which has flown forth "living waters" stands forth as a proof of the reality of our Faith in a world which would destroy the supernatural. Jesus Christ did not hesitate to call attention to His stupendous miracles as being the proof of His Messianic mission. And we should not be averse to pointing out to those who have not the Faith the modern miracles of Lourdes. Our Blessed Mother, and Bernadette herself in a lesser degree, might well address to us the words of our Lord:

The works themselves, which I do, give testimony of Me that the Father hath sent Me (John 5:36).

7

Bride of the Crucified

CATHERINE OF SIENA

CATHERINE BENINCASA smiled at herself in the long mirror. She admired the long gown whose shimmering folds fell in graceful lines down almost to the ground. She was fond of this gown, the first grown-up dress she had ever worn. Her father, Giacomo Benincasa, the dyer, had applied the rose-petal shade to the cloth with skilled hands; her mother had fashioned the dress with consummate art. This was the first time she had ever thus arranged the long, golden braids of her hair too, and the precarious task had been accomplished only with the aid of her favorite sister, Bonaventura. Catherine took up the tiny box of rouge: "Do I have to put this on my face?" she asked.

"Yes, my dear," answered her sister, "all the young women do, and if you want to win the heart of a gay young Signor, you had better, too."

"But I don't really want to win any young man," Catherine replied, "and I am only going to this festival because mother and father — and you — have insisted that I do. They say that I must get over my shyness."

The two young women laughed excitedly as the deft fingers of the elder sister applied the rouge to the fair skin of Catherine. Now the task of dressing was finished and she stood away a little from the mirror and surveyed herself. Her eyes shone lustrous and sparkling with eagerness. She tilted her head so that the light from the candles caught the soft curve of her cheek and the red fullness of her lips. With the aid of a smaller mirror she looked at her profile. "Yes," she admitted with the straightforward frankness and simplicity that characterized her, "I am beautiful."

Then the hand holding the small hand glass dropped to her side, and she turned full face to the long mirror. Her eyes glanced once again over her reflected image from tip of her shining slippers to top of her newly crowned head. Then her eyes met in the mirror, wavered, turned aside.

A small voice was saying within her heart: "Catherine, Catherine, are you going to turn aside from Me for such trifles?" She shook her head impatiently, and said to herself: "It is the wish of my mother and father, not mine, that I go to the festival. I am not the least bit interested in capturing a handsome young Signor. I am merely being obedient to them." And lest her keen mind detect the weakness in this manner of reasoning she quickly put the matter aside. Instead, the tiny voice was drowned in the music of the refrain that sang in her young, feminine heart: "The festival, the festival . . . music, singing, dancing, and perhaps . . . romance."

Catherine was born at Fontebranda in Siena on March 25, 1347. She was the twenty-third, and last, child of the dyer, Giacomo Benincasa and Lapa, his wife. March 25 is the Feast of the Annunciation of the Blessed Virgin Mary, and it seemed that heaven wished to celebrate the announcement of our Lady's virgin birth in a special manner by ushering into life this child who was to be marked out in such an extraordinary way by the love of Mary and her Son, Jesus. This child, Catherine, was to become the most dominating personality in the Italy of her time, and one of the most attractive feminine personalities of all times.

Catherine grew up a merry and lively child. She was strong and fleet of foot, earning by these excellences quite a reputation among her companions. Her sunny and happy disposition made her, from her earliest years, the petted idol of the whole neighborhood. Everybody loved her, and the laughing little tot with the golden curls was continually being stolen away (or borrowed, as the culprits would say) to spend the day at some neighbor's house. At a very tender age she was nicknamed *Euphrosyne,* which means *Lovely,* and this name remained with, and represented her, for life.

Heaven had marked little Catherine as its own from the first moment of her entrance into this world. She was always a lively playmate, and she loved games — but she found even greater delight in praying with all the earnestness of her child's heart to our Lady and to her sweet Jesus.

It is the year 1352. Catherine is now six years old, quite a capable little maid, and her mother allows her to go with her brother Stefano, a lad two years her senior, to spend the day with their married sister at the other end of the town. They are on their way home. Both are tired and are trudging up the hill toward the Benincasa house without a word. Suddenly Catherine stops. Her eyes are lifted and she is gazing across the valley in the direction of the Church of the Dominicans. Above the roof of this church she sees a wonderful jeweled throne, a kingly throne, in the sky, and on it is seated Jesus Christ, the Saviour of mankind. He is clothed in the full splendor of pontifical raiment, and on

His head He wears the triple crown of the Sovereign Pontiff — such as one would see on the head of Pius XII in Rome on the great day of a canonization. At His side are the Apostles Peter and Paul and St. John the beloved disciple. The little girl stands stock still, struck with the deepest wonder. She gazes with all her heart and soul in her eyes at her Kingly Lord, who has appeared in splendor and beauty to win her love. Jesus, her sweet Jesus, as Catherine so beautifully called Him, smiles and stretches forth His right hand and makes the Sign of the Cross over her.

So wonderful was the vision, and so full of sweetness was the blessing from the hand of the Son of God that Catherine was wholly oblivious of all that went on about her. She remained rooted to the spot in the open street, disregarding the traffic of men and beasts, until her brother Stefano, by now quite frightened at her strange behavior and her prolonged insensibility, pulled her by the arm and screamed:

"Catherine, what is the matter with you? Why don't you come?"

The girl seemed to awaken from a trance. She looked at Stefano, then gazed again in the direction of the Church of the Dominicans, but the vision was gone. Stefano wondered why his little sister wept so bitterly the rest of the way home, and why she upbraided herself for looking away. Thus did Christ first lay His hand in visible manner upon Catherine Benincasa to mark her for His own sweet bride.

Giacomo Benincasa was a very religious man. He was remarkable for his mild disposition and patience. From him Catherine inherited her unfailing gentleness and her natural piety. He was very strict about one matter in particular. He would not allow the least thing that savored of godless or ribald talk, either among the members of his own family or among his employees. Lapa was just the opposite of her mild-mannered husband, being energetic and quick of tongue and temper. Nor was she so inclined to religious observances of prayer and fasting and almsgiving as her husband and youngest child. But in spite of all this she was a very lovable wife and a most tender and devoted mother. It was from her that Catherine derived her great energy and power of decision and leadership.

Out of the vision of Jesus on the Via del Costone began a transformation of Catherine's whole spiritual life. A voice had spoken in her soul, "Come, follow Me," a voice like distant fairy bells that draw one on almost involuntarily to seek the wonderland whence they come. From now on Catherine sought out her little hermit's cave in the form of dark hiding places in hidden corners of the huge house, where she might pray. There she would kneel in prayer; there she would make her little fasts while the rest of the family were at their meals; there she would whip her small shoulders with a scourge of cords she had fashioned. She taught this game of holiness to other girls of her age, composed their prayers, and acted as their director. Her dominant personality, destined in later years to influence princes, prelates, and even the Pope himself, was already manifesting itself. She was in earnest. This was not make-believe for her. She was being a monk in the desert places and cloistered cell of her own home.

Catherine had now reached the age when a Sienese girl must think of a husband. Monna Lapa urged her to arrange her hair more becomingly, and to pay more attention to the young gallants who left no doubt that they desired to pay court to the youngest daughter of the Benincasa family.

Catherine would hear nothing of men. She was not interested in them. She would run away if a man ever entered the room. This irritated Monna Lapa who would scold: "Good heavens! They're not poison." Finally, Giacomo and Lapa managed to persuade Catherine to waver in her resolve. She would make herself attractive, she would allow her natural, vivacious charm to manifest itself. Although Catherine had not slackened in the deep spirituality which was hers since childhood, and though she still continued to regard herself as belonging to Jesus alone, yet she was a young woman — and like every normal young woman she had instincts for happiness, gaiety, and the swift movements of youthful life; she had the same desires of a home of her own, of a strong, tender husband with whom, hand in hand, she might walk through life, of many little faces that would look into her own and call her "mother." After all, marriage was a vocation, a career, too, and it was the springtime of her life, and singing in her blood and echoing in her heart was the God-given yearning for a life companion. Perhaps God intended her to serve Him in the wedded state. She was not sure but that disobedience in this wish of her parents that she marry might not gravely displease her Lord. So, she yielded a bit. Wearing her new dress, her face rouged, and her hair done up maturely, Catherine went to the festival, danced and sang and had a gay time. Not even then did she want a young Signor of her own.

The period of Catherine's enjoyment of the carefree life of the world was a brief one. It came to an end in 1362 with the sudden death of a sister dear to her heart, the beloved Bonaventura. The young woman wept beside the lifeless body and promised herself that never again would she turn aside from the service of her Master for the short-lived pleasures of earth, not even for the slightest moment spent in the enjoyment of worldly distractions. They were not meant for her. She belonged to Jesus, her Lord, and with renewed fervor of love she gave herself to Him. Bitter were the tears she wept over what she severely termed her apostasy from her chosen Spouse when she, like a dauber of bad taste, had tried to improve upon the work of the Divine Artist by applying cosmetics to her face — and that, in her vanity, to draw admiring eyes upon herself.

But Catherine's family was of just the opposite opinion. They were more determined than ever that their Euphrosyne marry. Indeed, a young man of influential family, and quite acceptable to the Benincasa household, desired to have her for his wife. But Catherine refused. Giacomo and Monna Lapa begged Fra Tommaso della Fonte, their adopted son, and lifelong companion of Catherine, to persuade her to marry. The young Dominican came to see Catherine — and she unburdened her heart to him. She told him of the vow of virginity she had taken, and declared firmly and decisively that she would love only one bridegroom forever, and that was Jesus Christ. Fra Tommaso listened to his little foster sister in speechless wonder at the purity of her soul, and the singleness of purpose she manifested of belonging to Christ alone. Instead of advising her to give in to her family and marry, he encouraged her to follow the voice of the Holy Spirit without deviating an inch from the path He indicated.

"Catherine," he said, "I think that you should leave no

doubt about your firm intention of never marrying; otherwise young suitors will be following at your heels for many years yet to come, and your family will insist more and more that you take a husband. As a result, life will become unbearable, and you will be prevented by such unwelcome attentions from giving yourself in wholesouled service to our Lord.

"I would advise you," he continued, "to cut off your hair, for that is the sign in the Catholic Church that a woman has given herself to God."

Catherine took this advice literally, and cut off her long, golden hair. But now she dreaded to face Monna Lapa, so she tried to conceal her closely cropped yellow head beneath a white kerchief which she wore like the veil of a nun. Lapa, however, was too keen not to notice the shorn locks of her child. She was very angry with Catherine and insisted more strongly than ever: "You shall have a husband. Your hair will grow out again, and then you will marry." Poor Monna Lapa! She and her daughter were poles apart in their respective temperaments; the mother could not understand the holy folly of her child. When Catherine cut off her beautiful hair it was the last straw. Something must be done, and quickly! "Too much piety — prayer and solitude — is the cause of this unreasonable and unnatural attitude," the mother decided. Thus it was determined in family council that Catherine should be given no time to exercise these holy arts of hers. She should take the place of the housemaid and do her tasks. That would keep her busy; that would shame her into submission. Catherine was consequently deprived of her own room, and became the maidservant. Her kind and loving family tried to be cruelly hard on their Euphrosyne because they loved her so dearly, and because they believed that this was the only way to make her see the light that would lead to her future happiness. They sincerely loved her and to hurt the darling of their hearts caused them poignant pain.

As for Catherine, this new arrangement began a period of almost unbearable joy and happiness, for she delighted in her new station. Far from being offended or humiliated she eagerly went about the performance of her daily tasks. The secret of her manner of turning her hard and lowly status into what she did, lay in the supernatural attitude with which she accepted it. She pretended that she was in the holy house of Nazareth; her gentle father was Jesus Christ, her mother was the Blessed Virgin; her brothers were the Apostles, and the journeymen who worked for her father were the relatives and friends of our Lord.

She no longer had a room of her own where she might go to pray, but she found an ally in her brother Stefano, who whispered to his little sister that she was welcome to use his room as her very own. Here it was that one day her father discovered her as she knelt in prayer, her spirit absorbed in union with God. He came in search of Stefano. Opening the door, he was about to step into the room when he noticed his darling Euphrosyne kneeling motionless near the far wall, with her gaze fixed upon an image of her crucified Saviour. His startled eyes next saw a beautiful white dove, which had been poised above the head of his daughter, turn in fright at his entrance and fly out the open window. Giacomo approached his Catherine, took her gently by the hand and raised her to her feet. She seemed to have been roused from a deep dream.

"My child," he asked, "where did you get that dove which was in the room when I entered?"

"What dove, father?" was the surprised query of his daughter.

Giacomo went directly to Monna Lapa and told her of the incident. He had long been convinced of the undeniable sincerity and holiness of his little girl. Now he was sure that the dove he had seen represented the Holy Ghost. The result of his conference with his wife was that Catherine should be allowed to have her own will with regards to a husband. Henceforth she should follow the inspiration of the Spirit of God without hindrance from her family. In the presence of the entire family Giacomo said to Catherine:

"God keep us from opposing His holy will, my child. Keep your vow of virginity, and live as the Holy Spirit directs you. We ask one thing only of you, that you pray always for us to your bridegroom, Christ. Never could we get a mightier one for you than He."

Catherine now had a small room — a bare cell was all it was — on the ground floor. The furniture consisted of a small wooden table, a stool, and wooden bench which served as her bed. Lapa would insist that her daughter sleep with her in her own warm, soft bed, but it was impossible to keep Catherine there for the whole night. She would wait until her mother slept, then rise and go down to her little room, where, if she slept at all, it would be on her bench. Lapa finally threw up her hands in surrender and let her strong-willed daughter remain in her room on the ground floor all the time. Catherine was happy nowhere else. On the wall hung a crucifix, the dearest possession of her heart. Here she

spent all her spare time, and the bare, cramped cell was trans-
formed by the ecstatic young woman into a lovely garden,
an antechamber to heaven. This was really what it was, for
she often enjoyed the company of heavenly visitors. Our
Lord Himself came often to visit her, bringing with Him
His own sweet Mother Mary, and John, Peter, Paul, and
Magdalen. Catherine talked and laughed with them, and she
shed tears, something which they could not do with her, for
their tears had been wiped away forever. She often heard the
singing of the blessed in heaven and would stop, wherever
she was, and say:

"Do you hear the singing? How beautiful it is!"

On one occasion she listened, then burst out:

"Hear St. Magdalen, how high and beautiful her voice is.
I hear her singing above all the rest."

Now it was that Catherine realized the ambition she had
so long cherished. She was received into the organization of
the Sisters of Penance of St. Dominic, or as they were called
in Siena, the Mantellate. They were generally known by this
latter title because of the white robe and black mantle they
wore. The Mantellate were not nuns in the strict sense of
the word, but were women who, in their own homes, devoted
themselves to prayer and penance, and worked among the
poor and nursed the sick.

But now it seemed that God abandoned her and left her
to endure the most terrible trials of her life. Hell seemed to
burst loose and with all its fury to beat upon the citadel of
her soul. She suffered the most torturing temptations, temptations that rose out of the very root of her human nature.
Catherine was young and within her blood the fever of
passion ran high as it does in every normal person. The

fiercer the conflict waged the more did she trust herself to the protection of her loving Lord, even though He seemed to be far away. Finally, the culmination was reached in a dream she had. A handsome young man came to her bearing an exquisitely rich and beautiful gown which he strove to place over her head, saying:

"Catherine, why did you cut off your beautiful hair? Why won't you wear this silk and gold-worked dress instead of that rough one of prickly cloth, which tortures your tender flesh?"

The handsome young man coaxed her to give up the life she was following and to come along with him.

"I will give you love and happiness and everything a woman's heart desires."

She had made her vow of virginity before she was old enough to realize what she was giving up, the tempter continued. "Will you never know the joy of being led away from the altar with your arm firmly linked in that of a young husband? Will you never have children of your own? Don't you want to live a full life, a natural life?"

With a shudder Catherine tore herself away from the insidious, whispering voice. She cast herself down full length before her crucifix. "Thou alone art my Bridegroom. I have never desired anyone but Thee, as well Thou knowest," her anguished heart cried. Suddenly there was a rustling in the room and there stood before Catherine, in vision fair as the Spring morning, the Queen of Heaven. She, too, was bearing a beautiful dress, shining in splendid colors and gleaming with precious metals and gems. With a smile she placed it lovingly over the head of the young woman in token of her victory.

Once again Catherine had to undergo the tortures of revolting temptations of the flesh; hell's minions strove with all their power to gain the victory over her. In the swirling blackness of this nightmare she kept her eyes fastened upon her crucified Lord, and cast herself within His Heart. "Of myself I can do nothing, but I trust in our Lord Jesus Christ." Again and again she repeated the sweet name of Jesus. Once more the fury of the storm abated, and, like the sunlight breaking through clouds black with rain and lighting up the world once more, our Lord came to Catherine's cell. A brilliant light shone round Him and all His wounds were bleeding.

"Catherine, My daughter," He said.

"Oh, sweet Jesus, where were You while my soul was being so sorely tempted?" she asked.

"I was in your heart, Catherine, for I will not leave anyone who does not leave Me first."

"In my heart, dearest Jesus, in the midst of all the temptations and impure images?" she exclaimed in astonishment. "If You were with me why did I not see You? I saw nothing but uncleanness and filth, and felt nothing but sadness and bitterness, and it seemed to me I was full of mortal sin."

"Tell Me, My child," our Lord said, "did these thoughts, these images, cause you happiness or sorrow?"

"Why, sorrow, bitter sorrow, of course. I hated them."

"And why do you think you felt that way if not because I was present in your soul and kept all its gates closed so that no evil vision enter in. I was in your heart. You did not feel Me, but I was there with My grace."

Her Divine Lord then left Catherine alone with her beating heart. It was almost dawn; she was exhausted after her long struggle. Sleep stole over her, and, whispering words, "My daughter," "My child," she smiled happily and dreamed.

Siena was rocked with the carnival uproar. The streets were crowded with masqueraders. Everywhere was the sound of music, of laughing voices. Wine flowed in great rivers these days; kisses were given and taken with free abandon; sin stalked abroad behind the masks — and in the open. During these days of carnival rioting Catherine was praying without ceasing: "Lord, increase my faith." It was now the last day of the Mardi Gras, Shrove Tuesday. As she prayed, a brightness, like the sun in noonday brilliance, illuminated the darkness of her room. Of a sudden, standing a few feet from her, she saw her Lord Jesus and the Blessed Virgin Mary. St. John, too, was there, and St. Paul and St. Dominic. Advancing to Catherine's side, our Lady took the girl's hand and holding it out to her Divine Son, she asked Him:

"My Son, wilt Thou espouse Thyself to Catherine?"

In answer He drew forth a ring set with four glistening pearls and a diamond that shone like the morning star.

"Behold," He said, "I have espoused thee, and I solemnly keep My betrothal with thee and take thee for My bride in the faith — because thou hast renounced the world and all its pleasures for love of Me, seeking all your joy in Me alone."

And Jesus took the golden ring and placed it on the finger of His bride.

Her visitors had departed; the bright light gradually faded, but in the gloom of the little room the ring gleamed on Catherine's finger. She kissed it and gazed at it; it was for her eyes alone to look upon, and no one else ever saw it upon her finger.

The three years that Catherine spent in the silence and solitude of her out-of-the-way cell were such happy ones that she would gladly have remained there the rest of her short life. However, this was not God's will. He had destined her for a great mission. She was to let her light shine before men; she was to win souls to Christ by her active apostolate. Christ told Catherine that He wanted her to participate fully in the family life of her home once again. She was also to visit the sick and poor of Siena and care for them.

Catherine, like all strong personalities, had some bitter enemies during her lifetime. But she bore misunderstandings, opposition, and even calumnious attacks with the bravery and calmness of her Divine Model. These were the crown of thorns she had chosen in preference to the one of jewels that He had offered for her choice at the beginning of her active life.

But she also had many friends. Her holiness attracted men and women of all ages and states of life to seek her company. Sanctity, naturally speaking, can sometimes be quite unattractive. Such was not the case with Catherine Benincasa, for united with, or rather, enhanced by, holiness, was her extremely lovable and attractive natural charm — and her beauty, so virginal and pure. There was something so winning about her personality that few could resist her. She possessed a keen and merry sense of humor, a tender, affectionate, and sympathetic heart, and a simple untaught wisdom. During the time she worked among the poor and sick of Siena, a company, or family as she termed it, was forming about her. Catherine was almost the youngest of this group, but still, all called her "mother" — and she was mother to the little band, but even more, she was heart and soul.

Alessia Saraceni, a young widow, and Lisa Colombini, Catherine's sister-in-law, were her closest women companions. Several Dominicans had also associated themselves with her. They were Fra Tommaso della Fonte, her adopted brother and first confessor, Fra Bartolomeo Domenico and Fra Domenico Cafferini. Some years later was added Fra Raymond of Capua, who was to become her confessor, her dearest friend, and her biographer. Among the laymen who followed Catherine was Francesco de Malevolti, a youthful nobleman whom she had rescued from a sinful and wasted life. Then there were Neri di Landoccio, a young poet of Siena, Stefano Maconi, and Barduccio Carrigiani. Stefano Maconi was a man of joyous temperament and great purity of life; he was the most trusted with responsibilities of all Catherine's spiritual sons. Every one of her disciples loved her, and this love was for each a means of drawing nearer to God, such was the influence her sanctity exercised upon them.

Catherine worked many wonderful conversions among hardened and calloused sinners, but perhaps the most wonderful incident to relate in this regard is the one that has to do with her victory over the soul of Niccolo di Toldi, a young Perugian nobleman. Niccolo di Toldi had been condemned to the gallows for some imprudent words he had uttered, while drunk, against the powers who controlled the Sienese city government. He was almost out of his mind with hatred and despair, and he cursed God and man. Catherine heard of him and went at once to the prison. She was taken to the cell of the boy who was so touched by her gentle words, and so impressed by her beautiful character that he was changed at once from a cursing, wild-eyed criminal to a weeping lad who clung to Catherine, as to a mother, for comfort. The next day she accompanied him to the gallows, strengthened him to go bravely through his ordeal, and received his head into her lap when the knife severed it from the body. Kneeling there on the scaffold, bathed in his blood, she saw his soul ascending to heaven. Christ told Catherine that this soul had been saved, had in fact gone straight to heaven, without any merit of its own, but due solely to the prayers and tears of His bride.

One day in the year 1370, July 18, when Catherine was meditating in prayer on the words "Create a new heart in me and renew a right spirit within me," she earnestly besought her Saviour to take her heart from her and give her His own heart instead. She plainly saw her Spouse come to her and take her heart from out her bosom and depart with it. For several days she had no heart at all, neither her own nor His. Then Christ came again after some days and in His hand He was holding a heart, purple-red and flaming. This heart He placed in the wound in Catherine's side from which He had taken her own heart. "My daughter," He said, "the other day I took your heart. Now I give you Mine in return."

In the year 1374 the Black Death broke out in Siena. This terrible plague was sweeping over the whole of Italy, causing frightful sufferings and fearful mortality. Men and women would be attacked as they stood talking in the streets and would die before they could reach their homes. The toll of deaths each day was terrifying. The heavy death carts rumbled down the stone streets all day and all night, depositing their cargoes of dead bodies in great wide trenches outside the city wall. Catherine and her companions went out and worked where the plague was raging fiercest. She herself went into the most infected parts of the city, and with her own hands cared for those who were puffed and blackened with the malady. From house to house she went, nursing the sick, consoling the dying, and burying the dead. Fra Raymond and his brother Dominicans labored day and night bringing the comforts of the Sacraments to sick and dying. On several occasions during the plague siege Catherine manifested the solicitude and love she cherished for each of her spiritual children by commanding the sickness to "Begone!" when it had infected any one of them. Messer Matteo, the superintendent of the hospital Misericordia, and a close friend of the Saint, was attacked by the terrible symptoms of the Black Death as he was attending a patient. Catherine hurried to him as he lay dying and said:

"Get up Messer Matteo, this is no time to be lying in bed."

He rose completely cured and went back immediately to his work with the plague-stricken. Fra Raymond, too, was felled by the specter. He begged that Catherine be summoned, and when she came to his cot she laid her hand on the brow of the suffering man, knelt down at his side, and prayed. Life returned to the limbs of her father confessor. Soon he dropped off into a refreshing sleep and when he awoke he was perfectly well.

"Give thanks to God who has preserved your life," Catherine said, "and go, labor much for the salvation of souls."

Now it was that Catherine's supreme mission in life was

made known to her. All that had happened thus far was preparatory for the great task Divine Providence had destined her to undertake. She was to bring the Church out of its Babylonian Captivity; she was to raise her voice to restore peace and unity once again to the Mystical Body of Christ, the Church. She was overwhelmed at the thought of her own impotence, but Christ her Spouse assured her:

"It is not you who are to do these things, but I. You are the human means I will use. You are a poor, weak instrument by which the power and wisdom of God will be manifested, for God always uses the weak and puny to confound the strong and powerful of this world."

Upon Catherine was placed the tremendous responsibility of reconciling the Pope with Italy, and of bringing him back to Rome. Rome must once more become the city of the successors of St. Peter. Since 1305 the Popes had resided on the banks of the Rhone at Avignon, a period known in history as the Babylonian Captivity. Catherine must initiate the slow, laborious work of reformation in the Church — reformation of abuses that were sapping the life strength of Christ's Church.

To her the Pope was Christ on earth, "Sweet Christ on earth," she so often called him. She looked beneath all human weaknesses and saw only the exalted, divinely bestowed character and office of the Sovereign Pontiff. She wrote repeatedly to Gregory XI, begging him to act manfully, to rule and govern the Church with wisdom and discipline, and above all else, to return to Rome — otherwise Christendom would be disrupted and fall to pieces. The reputation of Catherine's holiness, of her more than worldly wisdom, of the miraculous favors that indelibly stamped her as the Bride of Christ Crucified, had long since reached the ears of the Pope. He wrote to assure her that every possible step was being taken to do what she urged. For he was convinced that she was the mouthpiece of the Lord Christ whom he, as Sovereign Pontiff, represented on earth.

It was at this time, when she was moving heaven and earth to effect the reformation in the body of the Church, and to restore the Popes to Rome, that her Divine Spouse placed His hands on her in another token of His great love. While Catherine was praying in the Church of Santa Christina in Pisa on Laetare Sunday, her Crucified Lord appeared to her. His five Sacred Wounds were shining with brilliant, blood-red rays which came down to the young woman on the floor, and pierced her own hands, feet and side through and through. Henceforth, until her premature death at the age of thirty-three, she bore on her body, though invisible to human eyes, the sacred stigmata of her Crucified Bridegroom. She was now twenty-nine years old. Nine years had elapsed since her betrothal to Christ, her sweet Jesus.

Finally, when disappointment after disappointment seemed to brand her mission as a failure, the Pope returned to Italy. However, Catherine had first to make the long journey to Avignon before this happened. She came in June, 1376, with a small band of companions to the city on the Rhone. There she had many long conferences with Gregory XI, about peace in war-torn Italy, about reform, about Rome, about the call of all Christendom to a new Crusade. The result of Catherine's visit was that Gregory prepared to return to Italy, but still he vacillated in the face of the storm of protests raised by the French Cardinals. Then, on September 13, after his spirit was steeled by a last audience he granted to the Sienese mystic, Gregory set out on the long, dangerous road to distant Rome, a journey from which he was never to return. Catherine had fulfilled her mission, but the storm clouds were gathering like birds of evil omen over the Church of Christ. The Pope made his entry into the Eternal City on January 17, 1377. Gregory dwelt at Rome until his death on March 27, 1378. On April 8, a new Pope was elected. He is known in history as Urban VI, the Pope under whom the great schism was to break out.

Pope Urban VI had alienated all the Cardinals, save one, by the stringency of his reform measures. Now they had retired to Anagni where they elected another Pope, Cardinal Robert of Geneva, under the title of Clement VII, on the pretext that Urban's election had not been lawful. The real Pope, Urban VI, surrounded by dangers on all sides, commissioned Fra Raymond, who was in Rome at that time, to write to Catherine and bid her come to the Holy City without delay. Once again she left Siena with her chosen band. She was received in audience by the Pope immediately upon her arrival. He asked Catherine to address the new Cardinals he had appointed. She spoke to them in words that inflamed their hearts with courage and loyalty. She reminded them of their duty to Christ and His Vicar, and exhorted them to do God's will and fear nothing.

These last months, while the Church of Christ was being torn and wrenched with internal strife and disorder, were a time of intense suffering for Catherine. She had labored without rest for the cause of her Bridegroom, Christ, and she bore sorrow after sorrow with a breaking heart. Her health had been severely strained by her prolonged fastings and harsh penances which she had unremittingly exercised since the time of her betrothal to her Lord. Now her strength was rapidly diminishing and she knew that the hour for which she had so long sighed, and so earnestly besought her Spouse, was near: she was soon to be released from the last trammels of flesh and earth, and be united with Him forever.

On the third Sunday in Lent, 1380, Catherine was praying in the Church of St. Peter when she had a strange vision. She saw a great ship being placed upon her shoulders. The weight of the vessel was so great that it crushed her to earth. She then understood that the ship was the Church, and that she was to give her life that it might be saved from wreck. From that moment it was evident to all her devoted followers that their "mother" was dying. She received Extreme Unction on the Sunday before the Feast of the Ascension of her Divine Bridegroom into Heaven. Supported in the arms of her beloved Alessia, and with eyes fixed on the Crucified One, she prayed for the storm-tossed Church, for Urban VI, for her beloved sons and daughters. Her ardent spirit inflamed all about her with love for God even while they wept to lose her. Catherine's soul burst out from her body and into the embrace of her Lord and Master, her Beloved, her Betrothed, her Bridegroom, Christ. It was Sunday, April 29, 1380, and she was thirty-three years old. She had died of a broken heart — a heart broken for grief and love: for grief at the sight of the sufferings of the Church of her Spouse; for love of the One she had served so faithfully, and whom she desired with every fiber of her being. She was in life, in death, and for eternity, the Bride of the Crucified.

8

Plucky Little Girl
EULALIA

IT IS almost dawn. Birds are stirring in their nests, their claws tightening from the morning chill, and hungry young ones are beginning to gape suggestively. Soon some brave chanticleer will crow, and slowly, slowly, the old Roman city of Merida will awaken. Look, here comes the first wood peddler, his donkey stumbling sleepily under the heavy load of scrubwood gathered from the neighboring hills. They plod steadily up the street and pass the forum without noticing a pair of blue eyes blinking at them from behind the pillars of the Hall of Justice. Eulalia has been waiting here for more than two hours. It seems to her that the sun will never come dancing in golden brilliance over the eastern hills. How many more hours, she wonders, will she have to wait before the court convenes and she can talk to the judge?

Eulalia is only twelve, but her years have been eventful ones. The Christians of the fourth century still had to burrow around underneath the earth like worms in order to hear Mass and receive the Body and Blood of their dear Christ. How often Eulalia had accompanied her father and mother and uncle to some out-of-the-way *casa*, descended innumerable steps and then, with only candlelight to guide them, hurried down long tortuous, passages until at last they came upon a little group of Christians huddled around an old man reading to them from one of the Evangelists. The few *torchères* lighting the low-vaulted room would leave monster shadows glowering from every corner like devils hating them or like wicked pagans waiting to martyr them. But Eulalia forgot these when she listened to Christ's lovely stories about the lilies of the field, and the sparrows, and the naughty boy who ran away from his kind father, and the nice shepherd who went after the lamb that had strayed.

One day the priest, putting his hand upon her curly head, smiled into her serious eyes and asked:

"You love Christ, don't you, Eulalia?"

Something welled up in her throat, and she could not answer.

"You know," the priest went on, "that He may ask you to prove your love for Him just as He proved His love by dying for you."

"How can I prove my love, Father?" Eulalia asked.

"Some day, dear, He may ask you to be His martyr."

From that moment Eulalia never doubted that she was going to die for Christ. Her mother smiled at first, but as the months went on and Eulalia talked more and more about martyrdom, it began to get upon her nerves.

"That is all very well, child," her mother would gently say, "but aren't you being a bit selfish? How would your father and I get along without you?"

Matters became more serious when Eulalia's father caught her one day kicking at an image of Apollo in the market place. It was on account of this episode and Diocletian's late edict that anyone not showing reverence to the gods of the

empire should be put to death, that Eulalia's father and
mother determined to take their daughter into the country.

Summer had already set in. It was late afternoon with an
August sunset bursting in grand profusion. A thousand golds
and reds rained like pentecostal fire from the skies. Eulalia,
at the moment, was sitting at the far end of a luxuriant
garden, gazing, like Narcissus, into a limpid pool. She seemed
to be watching the glistening insects dart to and fro on its
surface, but her thoughts were elsewhere. She was listening
to an inward voice.

"Have you forgotten Me, Eulalia?" it asked.

Eulalia remained ever so still.

"Have you forgotten you are to be My littlest martyr?"

Could it be that now, right now, she was to die for Him?
Eulalia gradually made up her mind. She had to get back to
Merida.

Eulalia looked very young as she trudged along beneath
the stars. No one had heard her rise or creep stealthily out
of the house, and now she was going to her martyrdom.
Legend has it that a band of angels served as her escort, and
that they sang hymns of joy on the way. Thus it came about
that Eulalia was waiting at the Hall of Justice before
daybreak.

"Is this the little girl that wanted to see me?" Dacian asked.

The guard nodded assent and brought Eulalia before the
judge.

"Yes, honorable sir, this is the young lady. She has been
waiting a good while."

Dacian took Eulalia's hand.

"Has someone been molesting you?" he asked.

"Oh, no, sir, I only came to tell you that I am not going to reverence Jupiter or Venus or Bacchus or any of your other gods. I am only going to worship Christ the true God."

A look of supreme discomfort came over the attendants' faces. What little Christian spitfire was this? They were intensely relieved, however, at Dacian's loud guffaw.

"Well, we shall see, we shall see," he said. "Claudius, bring us some salt and incense."

Eulalia bit her lip firmly and looked steadily into the magistrate's eyes. She did not deign to notice an image of Mercury who stood balanced on a pedestal close to her side.

When salt and incense had been brought and placed before the image, Dacian began to coax Eulalia to retract her statement and offer sacrifice, but she would only shake her head in determined refusal.

At last losing patience, the judge peremptorily ordered instruments of torture to be shown her. Her only response was to reach out and touch them.

"Look here," he finally blustered, "merely walk up and touch a little of that salt and incense with the tip of your finger, and I'll let you go."

Eulalia taking a step in the direction of the image, pushes it over, stamps on the sacred pagan incense and, *di immortales!* spits in the judge's face, as representing to her the summary of all this superstition, and the very tempter himself who wished to seduce her from her loyalty to Christ.

Such insufferable insolence could never go unpunished. Dacian, choking with rage ordered her body to be torn with hooks and lighted torches applied to the wounds.

Through all the torture Eulalia never weakened. She was listening to a Voice ringing in her heart, ringing softly like far-off bells that impel attention by their insistence. Prudentius tells us that her soul mounted to Heaven in the form of a dove, and that the executioners were so frightened that they fled away. God, pleased with His littlest martyr, covered the body and the whole forum where it lay with a mantle of snow, even though it was yet summer.

This is the way the story would be told you at Oviedo where Eulalia is honored as patroness. Skeptics may laugh and doubt if such occurrences ever took place, but whether or not they believe in the escort of angels and the snowfall in summer, they will at least have to admit that Eulalia was a mighty plucky little girl.

He Opened His Heart to Her

MARGARET MARY ALACOQUE

THERE were many events in the year 1671 and no one thought at the time that the entrance of the humble French girl, Margaret Mary Alacoque, into the convent of the Visitation nuns of Paray-le-Monial was of much importance. The nuns of the convent certainly did not think so. For the girl was strange, full of mystery, subject to long periods of apparent ecstasy. They could not understand her long prayers; to them she did not seem able to follow their rule of life. It was not strange that they did not understand her, for they knew but little of this young woman who was already far advanced in holiness.

Margaret Mary Alacoque was born on July 22, 1647. As a child she had loved prayer and solitude; God had drawn her and she had responded to His invitations. Her father died when she was only eight and she had then been sent to a convent school. While at school she contracted a strange form of paralysis and was confined to her bed for four long years. But she was cured miraculously of this strange disease after she had dedicated herself to the Blessed Virgin and promised one day to be one of her daughters.

As childhood passed into girlhood God drew her ever nearer to Himself and sent her, in greater abundance, His gift of suffering. Both she and her mother fell into the hands of officious relatives and so great was their power over them both, that life for Margaret Mary became a constant torture. These relatives lived with Margaret Mary and her mother for years; they were years of suffering. Frequently, for days at a time, the young girl would stay outside the house in the garden weeping and praying, and when she re-entered the house, as she herself tells us, "it was with such fear and trembling that I seemed to myself like a poor criminal about to receive her sentence of condemnation."[1]

When she came to womanhood, marriage was suggested to her. Her mother begged her, with tears and sobs, to marry that they both might escape from the hands of their relatives. The devil, too, attempted to make her believe that if she entered religion she would make a laughingstock of herself. Thus Margaret Mary was torn between devotion to her God and devotion to her mother. The world, moreover, with all its pleasures, was an alluring temptation.

At the age of twenty-two she received the sacrament of Confirmation and this new influx of grace strengthened her. Soon after our Lord Himself appeared to her, as she herself tells us.

One day after Communion He showed me, if I am not mistaken, that He was the most beautiful, the wealthiest, the most powerful, the most perfect, and the most accomplished amongst all lovers. After having pledged myself to Him for so many years, how came it, said He, that I now sought to break with Him for another. "Oh! be assured that, if thou dost Me this wrong, I will abandon thee forever; but, if thou remainest faithful to Me, I will never leave thee, I Myself will be thy victory

---

[1] *Life of St. Margaret Mary, Written by Herself.* Trans. of the authentic French text by Sisters of the Visitation, Roselands, Walmer Kent (Visitation Library, 1930), p. 24. The various quotations throughout the present account are taken from this.

over all thy enemies. I pardon thy ignorance because as yet, thou dost not know Me; but, if thou art faithful to Me and followest Me, I will teach thee to know Me, and I will manifest Myself to thee."

This decided her. Nothing could change her. She would be a nun, and a nun of the sisters of the Visitation order of the convent of Paray-le-Monial.

Such was the history of this young woman whose prayers were so fervent and whose devotion was so apparent, but her sisters in religion did not know these things and to them she seemed a visionary. This caused Margaret Mary untold mental suffering. Her physical suffering, too, was almost continual and of such a nature that the doctors could make nothing of it. Doubtless, she must have seemed to many to be a hypochondriac.

It was this humble woman, thus prepared by years of suffering and long and earnest prayer, literally burning with love for her God, to whom Christ was to reveal Himself and His love for her sake and for ours. But before we read her message we must prepare ourselves.

For a moment let us forget the daily press blazoning forth the most recent divorce or the latest murder, the rhythmic purr of the radio at our elbow, the streamlined car as it streaks past — let us forget these things and face the true realities, the profound realities, the realities which must mean something to us.

Man was made for God and by God. More than this, God gave to man a life above his natural life, a life of Sanctifying Grace by which man could merit eternal rewards and the privilege of seeing God face to face in the life to come. It was a free gift. It was given to Adam; it was lost by Adam, and through him, we, his children, lost our inheritance. But God so loved us that He willed to give His only Son for us. "By this hath the charity of God appeared toward us, because God hath sent His only-begotten Son into the world, that we may live by Him. In this is charity: not as though we had loved God, but because He hath first loved us, and sent His Son to be a propitiation for our sins" (John 4:9). Christ, then, came into this world, suffered and died upon a cross that we might again have this supernatural life. He instituted an organization, the Catholic Church, to furnish men the means of obtaining and increasing this life.

There have been additional aids offered to men by God during the centuries; for example, devotion to particular saints;[2] the institution of religious orders peculiarly adapted to meet the problems of their day and those of succeeding years; or the special devotions to Mary the Mother of God. These helps might be regarded as "short cuts" to sanctity. They are not essential; but they are certainly important.

The devotion which was revealed to Margaret Mary was probably the most important of these helps. It came to a Catholicism warped by Jansenism, to a Christendom weakened by Protestantism, to a Europe which would soon stagger on from the sectarian strife of the seventeenth century to the vague Deism of the eighteenth. It was sent to strengthen in men that supernatural life which is all important. Let us learn of it in Margaret Mary's own words. We see her in the

[2] Devotion to the saints is really a very common-sense affair. If a man desires a job he will, if he can, use the "pull" or influence of his friends to help him. The saints have a "pull" with God. We ourselves are often weak and sinful; we need someone who has a "pull" with God to help us. So we pray to the saints to ask God on our behalf.

convent chapel praying before the Blessed Sacrament. In her own words:

One day, having a little more leisure — for the occupations confided to me left me scarcely any — I was praying before the Blessed Sacrament, when I felt myself wholly penetrated with the Divine Presence, but to such a degree that I lost all thought of myself and of the place where I was, and abandoned myself to this Divine Spirit, yielding up my heart to the power of His love. He made me repose for a long time upon His Sacred Breast, where He disclosed to me the marvels of His love and the inexplicable secrets of His Sacred Heart, which so far He had concealed from me. Then it was that, for the first time, He opened to me His Divine Heart in a manner so real and sensible as to be beyond all doubt, by reason of the effects which this favor produced in me, fearful as I always am of deceiving myself in anything that I say of what passes in me. It seems to me that this is what took place: "My Divine Heart," He said, "is so inflamed with love for men, and for thee in particular that, being unable any longer to contain within Itself the flames of Its burning Charity, It must needs spread them abroad by thy means, and manifest Itself to them in order to enrich them with the precious treasures which I discover to thee, and which contain graces of sanctification and salvation necessary to withdraw them from the abyss of perdition. I have chosen thee as an abyss of unworthiness and ignorance for the accomplishment of this great design, in order that everything may be done by Me."

On one of the first Fridays while Margaret Mary was praying before the Blessed Sacrament our Lord presented Himself to her and she tells us:

It was then that He made known to me the ineffable marvels of His pure (love) and showed me to what an excess He had loved men, from whom He received only ingratitude and contempt. "I feel this more," He said, "than all that I suffered during My Passion. If only they would make Me some return for My love, I should think but little of all I have done for them and would wish, were it possible, to suffer still more. But the sole return they make for all My eagerness to do them good is to reject Me

and treat Me with coldness. Do thou at least console Me by sup-
plying for their ingratitude as far as thou art able. . . . In the
first place thou shalt receive Me in Holy Communion as often
as obedience will permit thee. . . . Thou shalt, moreover, com-
municate on the First Friday of each month.

The final great manifestation of Christ's love for us and
His invitation to each of us occurred on one of the days of
the Octave of Corpus Christi, probably in the year 1675.
Again let Margaret Mary tell us of the revelation:

> Being before the Blessed Sacrament one day of Its octave, I
> received from my God signal tokens of His love, and I felt urged
> with the desire of making Him some return, and of rendering
> Him love for love. "Thou canst not make Me a greater return of
> love," He said, "then by doing what I have so often asked of
> thee." Then, discovering to me His Divine Heart, He said:
> "Behold this Heart, which has loved men so much, that It has
> spared nothing, even to exhausting and consuming Itself, in order
> to testify to them Its love; and in return I receive from the
> greater number nothing but ingratitude by reason of their ir-
> reverence and scarileges, and by the coldness and contempt which
> they show Me in this Sacrament of Love. But what I feel the
> most keenly is that it is hearts which are consecrated to Me, that
> treat Me thus. Therefore I ask of thee that the Friday after the
> Octave of Corpus Christi be set apart for a special Feast to honor
> My Heart, by communicating on that day and making repara-
> tion to It by a solemn act, in order to make amends for the
> indignities which It has received during the time It has been
> exposed on the altars. I promise thee that My Heart shall expand
> Itself to shed in abundance the influence of Its divine love upon
> those who shall thus honor It, and cause It to be honored." And
> when I replied that I knew not how to accomplish what He had
> so long desired of me, He told me to address myself to His
> servant, whom He had sent me for the accomplishment of this
> design.

St. Margaret Mary did her utmost to fulfill our Lord's
command. Father de la Colombiére, S.J. — referred to as

"His servant" in the last sentence above — gave her every encouragement, and he himself was chosen by our Lord to aid in bringing to men this new message of God's love for them. And from Margaret Mary he received the message that it was Christ's wish that the Society of Jesus should make known the value and utility of this devotion. But in the September of 1676 Father de la Colombiére was sent to England and Margaret Mary had to carry on almost alone.

During the fifteen years of life that remained to her the Saint did her best to make the Sacred Heart known and loved. Her life of suffering continued and was increased as she saw the slowness with which others responded to her message. She worked on; she suffered on; finally, she saw the devotion take some hold in her own community. She knew that Father de la Colombiére had worked earnestly to make the Sacred Heart loved until his early death in 1682; she knew his work had not been in vain. The devotion had begun to spread; it was enough; her work was done.

On the evening of Tuesday, October 17, 1690, Margaret Mary lay dying in the convent of Paray. She had told the sisters that her death was near. They had doubted her at first, but now they knew she had spoken truly. As she lay there, her lifework a complete success, she said to her mother superioress:

"Mother, I have no longer need of anything but God alone, and to be hidden forever in the Heart of Jesus Christ."

It was a fitting summary of her life. She had even begged the infirmarian to destroy the pages, written under command of Holy Obedience, concerning herself and the graces God had given her. But yielding to the wishes of others, she had resigned this also to God. And so she died. She was only forty-three. Her doctor was firmly convinced that, since there was no apparent physical cause he could discover, the cause of her death was Divine Love. And so it may have been.

But this we know for certain that in the little town of Paray, on that Tuesday evening, died one to whom we, men and women of today, owe more than we can understand. Those who write of our civilization and of the history of nations, may never speak of her influence upon our world. Even if they wished, they could scarcely evaluate it. But in that most important history, the history of how men save or lose their souls, St. Margaret Mary's power and influence are undoubted. The hundreds of churches dedicated to the Sacred Heart, the solemnity of the Feast of the Sacred Heart in the Church, the thousands of confraternities, the millions of men and women who try in some way to offer reparation to the God who loves them so much, all these attest that she accomplished her work. The devotion to the Sacred Heart has become widely known and widely practiced, which is what Margaret Mary wished. She herself is known by comparatively few, which is also as she wished.

10

The Heroine of Cordova
FLORA

IT WAS the year 845 of our era. The day was hot, but not too hot to keep Cordova from attending the trial. Already every seat in the Hall of Justice was taken, though fully an hour before the judge would arrive. Viewed aloft from the dais, the room had the aspect of an oriental garden, brightly colored turbans bobbing restlessly like flowers in a breeze. Rich Moslem merchants were gesticulating wildly and frowning so fiercely that one surmised some personal interest in the trial. There were others of a poorer class, for the most part, who seemed sad and nervous. Gossips waited with keen expectancy. As a matter of fact, the case to be tried was of interest to everyone: to the wealthy Moslems, because the honor of their religion was being jeopardized; to the Christians, who had managed to slip in, because it meant that another of their number was about to be forced to prove her love for Christ; and to the gossips, who crowded into the places still left vacant, because the defendant's brother was to act as prosecutor.

The entrance of Moad ben Otma el Xabani, the judge, caused a little stir of excitement which soon subsided into silence. When he had taken his place on the dais, a door to the left opened. Again there was a rustle of excitement. Flora, radiantly beautiful, entered with two attendants. Hers was not the demure beauty that Christian art has led us to associate with sanctity, but a vigorous type of attractiveness. Dark eyes revealing great firmness of resolution, together with a decided animation of manner proved somewhat disconcerting to Moad and the court alike. She was told to sit down opposite her brother. The ghost of a smile played about her lips as she bowed to him. But ignoring her, he rose to his feet and began:

"Honorable cadi, my sister did not always scorn our holy prophet. She kept the rites of our religion faithfully and practiced its sacred customs. We lived in peace and happiness, but influenced by these Christian dogs, she ran away from home, and only strongly against her will did she return. She dared me, honorable cadi, to tear her Faith away from her. She said I could not separate her from Christ who she believes is God and whom she reverences now instead of Mohammed. I have beaten her, but she is stubborn. She boasts she will suffer anything for this Carpenter. Let us see!"

At this Moad's brow knit severely. Evidently this was more than could be tolerated. An earnest Moslem, he would show this young girl that she had but two alternatives, either to reject this Christian foolishness or to bear the punishment. But he would let her speak.

"Are these accusations of your brother true?" he asked her. She was silent. Moad continued.

"Do you not know that the daughter of a Moslem must be a Moslem or die?"

At this Flora rose, her lips quivering with indignation.

"I have never been a Moslem. Our mother was a Christian, and from my infancy I have known none but Christ. Outwardly, I admit, I used to keep the Moslem rites, but that was because I was weak, *weak*. When the muezzin called from the minaret, he, who calls himself my brother, thought I was praying to Allah, but I was praying to the God of Christians in my heart. Then I was weak, now I am strong, and I am ready to die for Christ, because I have consecrated myself to Him as His bride."

Moad, pitying Flora's youth and beauty, instead of ordering her death, believed that punishment would suffice to make her change her views. He had two men hold her arms while a third lashed her about the nape of the neck, wounding her delicate head and despoiling it of its beautiful locks. This torture was continued until Flora fainted. Then the judge ordered her brother to take her home, have her instructed in Mohammedanism, and if she still rebelled to bring her again before him.

Back in her brother's house, Flora found herself attended by members of his harem who were instructed to watch her most rigorously. She was not the type of person, however, to give way to difficulties. Although her severe wounds were hardly healed, she determined to get out of her brother's grasp. In the dead of night, she slipped into the patio and with the aid of some clinging vines climbed to one of the lower buildings. Crouched in the shadows, she waited on the roof to listen if anyone had been awakened by her hurried ascent. All was quiet. The long drop from the opposite side of the roof to the street below made her almost despair, but it was her only chance. Making the Sign of the Cross, she wormed over the edge, shut her eyes, and let herself fall. Unhurt, she ran until she came to the house of a Christian friend.

Days of hiding and pursuit followed. But Flora was so deeply in love with Christ that neither sufferings nor hardships mattered. She gloried in having endured the scourge of her Divine Spouse. She gloried in thus having been allowed to share in His holy Passion. She did not yet know that one day she should also mount the Cross.

Eulogius, a priest, happened to say a secret Mass at which Flora was present. He was struck by the wonderful reverence with which she received Holy Communion and afterwards inquired about her. On learning of her courage beneath the Moslem lash, he was filled with deepest admiration. Flora became for him the perfect type of Christian womanhood, and there sprang up between them a friendship which has its counterpart only in the spiritual love of Jane Frances de Chantal and Francis de Sales, of Theresa of Avila and John of the Cross. Throughout all his years, Eulogius looked upon Flora as a saint sent by God into his life to inspire him to greater Christlikeness. And she, in turn, was to find strength from his letters in moments when she needed strength badly.

Eulogius sent Flora to hide at Osera, a little town in the direction of Seville, while he himself remained to further Christianity among the fanatical Mohammedans of Cordova. One day while Flora was praying in the Church of San Acisclo she felt someone touch her lightly on the shoulder. Looking up, she beheld a palefaced girl of about her own age. Maria Walabonsus had recognized Flora as the one who had suffered so bravely for her Faith at Cordova and desired to talk with her.

In the deepening dusk, when night, like a dragon with

diamond eyes, was beginning to coil itself around the tired world, Flora and Maria walked together and talked of those things which were close to their hearts. Maria's home was in the mountains of Cordova, tall-wooded mountains that leaned like a purple rampart against the sky. Flora's mother had often described their majestic beauty, as she, too, lived among them as a girl. But Maria was not talking this evening of scenic splendor. She was telling Flora of her great sorrow. An elder brother, whom she loved dearly, had endured martyrdom with six others for their loyalty to Christ. The shock of this news had, at first, almost driven her to distraction, but her brother had appeared in vision and told her to cease weeping for soon she would be with him in Heaven. Martyrdom, now, seemed to be her only desire.

"Flora," she went on, "life is of worth to me now only in its losing. My brother will obtain for me the grace to face death as he did. Yesterday, after saying farewell to my little brothers and sisters, I set out for Cordova, whither I go now, to declare my belief in Christ before the Moslem judge Said ben Soleiman. You must pray for me. Pray that I will be as brave as you were. Oh, Flora, it seems that instead of fear, only impatient longings fill my breast. I could not bear it, if I should not be able to die for Christ."

Smiling, Flora took the poor girl into her arms. God, she knew, would not reject such ardent and generous love. While Maria had been speaking of martyrdom, a similar desire had been awakened in her own heart. With the animation characteristic of her, Flora proposed that they start at once together for Cordova in search of the Cadi.

Eulogius had already been in prison for two months.

Starved, half naked, sharing his food and corner with the prying rats, he still defied the Moslem's efforts to make him yield. Questioned as to the submission of the prisoner, the poor Arab appointed to guard Eulogius had always to confess, "He sings night and day to the Christian God." When they surrounded him with filth, bound him with chains, shut out all light, they did not know that the spirit of a saint is satisfied by other visions. Eulogius walked down the streets of Heaven beneath serene and snowy summits bathed in the white light of eternity. He conversed with Christ and his friends who had already suffered martyrdom. Praying, he spoke with them. Though the Moslem might prevent him from holding Christ in his hands at holy Mass, they could not prevent him from holding Christ always in his heart.

Late one afternoon the heavy door of the dungeon was opened and someone was cast cruelly in upon the floor. The door slammed to. Eulogius' eyes being accustomed to the darkness, he recognized the new prisoner as a fellow Christian.

"Hail, fellow sufferer for Christ!" Eulogius cried.

There was much joy between the two. The discomforts they experienced were forgotten in the love and admiration each Christian felt for the other. At the mention of Flora's name, Eulogius leaned forward eagerly.

"Has Flora come again to Cordova?" he asked.

"Yes, Eulogius, but the story is not altogether a happy one," replied the newcomer. "About a week ago we heard that some Christians were taken and were going to be brought before the cadi, so my brother and sister and I hurried to the Hall of Justice. Flora was already before the judge when we came in. Never did she seem more poised, more carefree. She answered the judge's threats with a smiling unconcern which completely dismayed, then angered, him. If we were proud of her defiance before, Eulogius, how can I tell you the joy that surged in every Christian breast, when, cool and with complete assurance, she affirmed that death was a mere trifle to pay for an eternity with Christ. She gave the impression that no matter what they did to her, they could not touch that part of her which was most truly herself."

Eulogius did not utter a word. But his eyes were shining with a new light. He urged his friend to proceed.

" 'Once before I was given over to you, honorable cadi,' she said, 'and suffered most cruelly at your hands. Since then I hid myself, because I was afraid — but today I come forward and assert more strongly than ever that Jesus Christ is the Son of God, and that Mohammed is a false prophet, an adulterer and an evildoer.'

"The silence that followed upon her words was so intense that one hardly dared breathe. It was a strange, ominous silence like the hushed expectancy immediately preceding the rise of the curtain on the last act of a tragedy, or like that moment of foreboding before a storm, when trees cease to whisper and birds to sing, and clouds, like frightened children, scurry noiselessly across the skies in search of some haven. Then suddenly the Hall was filled with a deafening tumult. The crowds, raising clenched fists, surged toward the front."

"Was Flora alone?" Eulogius broke in.

"No," replied his companion, "there was another girl with her, Maria by name, whose brother had already suffered martyrdom for the Faith. Rushing into Flora's arms, she cried out that she, too, believed Christ to be God, and, like Flora and her brother, was ready to die for this belief.

"Sternly, the cadi ordered that they be thrown into the same prison with women of bad repute, and threatened that if they did not change their minds he would sell them at the public market. This was a fate worse than death, since it meant prostitution and the life of the harem.

"Eulogius, here is the unhappy part of the story. Both Flora and Maria, so anxious to suffer death for Christ, are deeply troubled and confused at what course to follow. The persuasion of Flora's family, and the sordid immorality of the prison are beginning to weaken their resistance. We must pray, Eulogius, we must pray for their constancy."

Poor Eulogius! He could not imagine Flora, so noble, so brave, forsaking Christ. Was Moslemism to win her back? Obtaining writing material, he sent her a letter in which he tells her that as long as her soul is virginal even corporeal prostitution does not matter. It is a beautiful letter which belies the strong feelings of his heart. Having settled the doubt of the two virgins of Christ he addresses himself to Flora alone, as if in private with her who had special claims on his attention, and writes:

Now I will enter the port of silence. I have given you your weapons. And now, O most holy sister Flora, flourishing in virtuous merits, now I wish to speak to you for a little while, so that you may gladly remember my friendly words as the last counsels of a tender father and keep them in your holy mind and heart. "Hearken, O daughter, and see, and incline thy ear: and forget thy people and thy father's house. And the king shall greatly desire thy beauty: for He is the Lord thy God" (Ps. 44:11, 12). Your vocation is not that of others. With a wolf for a father and a lamb for a mother, you flourish like a lily among thorns.

11

She Kept the Secret of Her Queen
CATHERINE LABOURÉ

WE OFTEN hear it said that spoiled children never come from a large family. Perhaps that is why Catherine Labouré, whom the members of her family and her friends affectionately called Zoé, was such an unselfish, happy child. She was the ninth of eleven children born in the truly Catholic family of Pierre and Louise Madeleine Labouré.

Zoé was born at Fain-les-Moutiers, in Burgundy, France, not far from Bourbilly, the birthplace of St. Jane Frances de Chantal. Her birthday was May 2, 1806, and on the very next day her parents, in the best Catholic fashion, took her to the parish church to have her baptized.

Zoé had only two sisters, all the rest were brothers. All but one of these brothers were older than she. The best testimony that she was a lovable sister and a child of remarkable character comes from the fact that even her brothers — all without exception — said that everything she did was well and quickly done. That is praise indeed coming from eight brothers!

Zoé's mother died when she was only nine years old. Madame Labouré had trained her children in true and solid Catholic piety, and so it seemed the most natural thing in the world that when Zoé was left without an earthly mother, she instinctively and wholeheartedly turned to her heavenly

Mother. She intensified her devotion to the Mother of God, and had God's Mother for her own Mother during the rest of her long life. About this time she was once discovered standing on a table with her little arms embracing a statue of our Lady. Her Queen Mother had not as yet come to her, so she would, as it were, anticipate her visit, and by loving the image of the Blessed Virgin manifest the love of her child heart.

For two years or so, after her oldest sister had gone to be a Daughter of Charity of St. Vincent de Paul, Zoé lived with her Aunt Marguerite in the village of Saint Remy. At twelve she returned to Fain-les-Moutiers. Soon after her return she was overjoyed to assume the management of the household for her father, to cook for the farm hands, and to help in the raising of her younger brother. Not only her brothers but even the villagers recognized in Zoé and her sister, Antoinine, model housekeepers.

Zoé, indeed, was liked by all. Even the birds seemed to claim her as their friend. A favorite diversion for her was the care of pigeons in the farmyard. When she appeared hundreds of her feathered friends gathered around and circled over her head, as if to crown her with an aureola symbolic of her innocence and purity.

At this time, too, she received her First Holy Communion. Her sister said that from her earliest years, but more especially from the time she made her First Holy Communion, Zoé cherished a childlike love for the Blessed Virgin. From the humble Victim in the Sacred Host she evidently learned to love humility and was later to learn how to imitate His silence and obscurity.

While here in Paris she sought the advice of her older sister, now Superioress of one of the houses of Charity in southern France. Sister Mary Louise replied in a letter that perfectly described the high vocation of a Daughter of Charity. It was this letter that weighed down the scales and made Catherine follow her vocation no matter what the opposition.

To return to the subject of our vocation. Would that I might give you even a slight idea of its advantages! What is it to be a Daughter of Charity? It is to give oneself without reserve to God for the service of His poor, His suffering members, to console the unfortunate, to be the spiritual mothers of innocent children whom unnatural parents have abandoned, to care for the afflicted, to visit the sick, and to prepare the dying to meet a merciful Saviour.

What a calling! Nothing less than to imitate the life of Jesus Christ who went about doing good. Is it not to be, as it were, messengers of His mercy, dispensers of His charity, showing forth His divine attractions, drawing from His Sacred Heart sentiments of devotedness and love especially in favor of the little children with whom He charges us, as His apostles of charity?

A proof that she had long since pledged herself to God was also afforded by the fact that she refused many attractive offers of marriage.

Her earnestness and perseverance in prayers overcame the objections of her father. He finally yielded to the entreaties of his daughter-in-law, Madame Hubert Labouré, who pleaded with him to allow his second daughter to join the family of St. Vincent de Paul. Early in January, 1830, Zoé, now to become Sister Catherine, began her probation of three months at Chatillon-sur-Seine.

One of the nuns who had been with her in these first days of her probation later heard that the Blessed Mother had appeared to one of the Sisters of the community in which

Sister Catherine was living at the time. So favorable and lasting was the impression the young religious had made on her during this period that the nun remarked:

"If the Blessed Virgin has manifested herself to a Sister of the seminary, surely it must have been to Sister Labouré. That child is destined to receive great favors from heaven."

During the time of probation her sweet, joyous personality shed its light on all about her. On April 21 she was thence sent to the Seminary of the Daughters of Charity, situated on the Rue du Bac, Paris. Here, while still in her novitiate, it was that the great favors we shall shortly note were to be conferred on her and she was to acquire the title by which she is known today, "The Seer of Rue du Bac."

It was during these days that she began to be favored with the visible presence of our Lord in the Blessed Sacrament. This happiness, she tells us, was hers throughout the whole course of her seminary training, except on rare occasions when slight shadows of doubt as to our Lord's visible presence crossed her mind. On June 6, 1830, Trinity Sunday, according to her testimony, she beheld in vision, Christ the King.

But these extraordinary graces were merely preliminary and preparatory, as it were, to the remarkable visions of the Blessed Mother of God, and the important mission for her connected with them. Thrice our Lady came to speak to her in the most intimate terms, to reveal to her the desires of her Immaculate Heart and her plans for the devotion of the Miraculous Medal. With the utmost simplicity Sister Catherine has written, at the command of her confessor, the history of these wonderful revelations, stating simply that she had long entertained an ardent desire of seeing the Blessed Virgin.

Here, then, is the story as told by her.

On the eve of the feast of her Father St. Vincent, Sister Catherine had gone to sleep with a prayer to the Saint that he might obtain for her the favor of beholding the Blessed Mother. It was eleven thirty by the clock on July 18, 1830. Suddenly a child, whom she later identified as her Guardian Angel, came and called her to say that the Blessed Mother awaited her in the chapel. Three times the same call was repeated. She arose, and when she arrived at the chapel she found it ablaze with the splendor as of a Midnight Mass. Presently, after waiting with her a short time in the sanctuary, the child again spoke.

"There," it said, "is the Blessed Virgin."

Sister Catherine turned. It was the Mother of God herself whom she saw at the foot of the altar!

What next ensued she tells us in her own straightforward style:

Then casting a glance at the Blessed Virgin, I sprang forward, throwing myself on my knees on the steps of the altar. I rested my hands on the knees of the Blessed Virgin. At that instant I tasted the sweetest joy of my life, a delight beyond expression. Then it was that she told me how I was to act toward my director and revealed to me many other things which I am not at liberty to disclose.

Imagine the Blessed Virgin visiting you, allowing you to rest your hands on her knees while you kneel at her feet! Imagine your heart and soul filled to overflowing with this inexpressible joy that Catherine speaks of, and then imagine yourself if you can, telling this to no one but your confessor during all the rest of your life! Yet that is exactly what this saintly nun did, out of humility and a desire to be unknown, for the love of God.

The priest to whom she revealed these favors, at first — and with good reason — merely disregarded them. He simply told her to practice true devotion to the Blessed Mother. In all that was related to him he saw what seemed to him no more than the imaginings of a pious soul. But Mary herself had forewarned Sister Catherine that at first her confessor would disregard her visions. So the good nun quietly went about her ordinary daily duties until again God's Blessed Mother came to her.

It was on November 27, of the same year, that Sister Catherine was favored with her second vision of our Lady. The Sister had been convinced that she would see the Blessed Virgin "in the perfection of her beauty," and she was not to be disappointed. Our Lady now appeared to her in the attitude and manner made familiar to us all, by her image on the Miraculous Medal. Among other things, the Queen of Heaven told her that God wished to confide to her a special mission. Here are the good Sister's words, who herself has since received from the Church the title of "Blessed." They give the details as a woman would naturally tell them:

I saw the Blessed Virgin. . . . She was clothed in white. Her robe of silk, of auroral whiteness, was fashioned in the style termed *a la vierge,* high neck, and plain sleeves. Beneath a white veil which fell to her feet, and resting ligthly on the hair was a fillet with a lace edging about an inch in width. The figure was distinctly outlined. The feet rested upon a sphere, or rather a half sphere, as only half was visible. Her attitude was natural and graceful; her eyes directed heavenward . . . the whole figure resplendent with beauty, such beauty as I cannot describe. . . . At this moment I scarcely knew where I was. All I can say is that I was immersed in supreme delight, when a panel of oval shape formed around the Blessed Virgin and on it, traced in golden letters, were these words: "O Mary conceived without sin pray for us who have recourse to thee!" Then a voice said to me: "Have a medal struck on this model. All those who wear it will receive great graces. It should be worn around the neck; great graces will be the portion of those who wear it with confidence. . . ." All at once the picture seemed to turn and I saw the reverse of the medal.

This, then, is the mission for which Mary was choosing the humble Daughter of Charity. She was to give to the world this further proof of our Blessed Mother's love and solicitude for the whole world and for each individual soul. And it was to be revealed in a manner intelligible to all, in a manner tangible, visible. The Miraculous Medal would show man the Mother of God herself showering down graces on souls the whole world over, symbolized by the rays of light that fell from her hands and covered the globe on which she stood. The perfection of beauty of the Mother of God would draw all hearts to her, even as it filled with supreme delight the heart of Sister Catherine.

Once more, she kept her secret inviolate. Her confessor only was to know as yet. It was a secret between herself and her Queen.

But still a third time the Heavenly Mother came to her and repeated the great commission. Again her confessor regarded it all as only the fond imaginings of a devoted client of the Blessed Virgin. Besides, Sister Catherine had exacted from him a formal promise never to reveal her name or identity. Thus giving further proof of her humility. The mission to which she was dedicated should be carried out, but no one was to know of her relation to it. Once only in her long subsequent life did she ever give the slightest hint that she was the privileged soul to whom these manifestations had been made. It was when a nun of her community playfully remarked in the presence of Sister Catherine that surely "the Sister who believed she had seen the Blessed Virgin had only beheld a picture."

"My dear," replied Sister Catherine, in unmistakable tones, "the Sister who saw the Blessed Virgin saw her in the flesh just as we see each other."

After these words she dismissed the subject and lapsed into her customary and inviolable silence about the heavenly visitations.

Following upon the third and last apparition, our Blessed Mother spoke to her interiorly. "My daughter," she said, "henceforth you will see me no more, but you will hear my voice during meditation." Shortly after, she told the Sister to try more earnestly to have the medal struck. The saintly nun humbly replied that her confessor would not believe her, and how then could she hope to fulfill our Lady's wishes if he would give no credence to the visions. She was assured in turn that her confessor, being a true servant of God, would finally do what the Blessed Mother wished.

So it came to pass that, in 1832, Father Aladel had the medal struck. It was approved by his superiors and the marvelous effects that followed soon caused it to be popularly called the Miraculous Medal. That is its title today, and it is worn by thousands upon thousands of devoted children of the Queen of Heaven, who probably never have even heard the name of Catherine Labouré. Indeed the devotion never

It was during the closing days of the Sister's life, some forty years after the apparitions, that she was passing down the hall of the house of the Sisters of Charity at Enghien, engaged as usual with her own tasks.

"There is the Sister of the apparitions of 1830," whispered a young nun to a friend who was visiting her.

"My dear Sister," exclaimed the young lady as she quickly caught up with Sister Catherine, "how charmed I am to meet the one so highly favored by the vision of the Miraculous Medal!"

The old Sister replied with merely a smile and a look of utter astonishment. The young nun now realized her imprudence, and tried to correct the fault by explaining to her friend that Sister Catherine wished to remain unknown. That evening she went to apologize to Sister Labouré. In doing so she supplied another evidence as to how well the holy religious had concealed for nearly half a century the wonderful privileges of which she was the recipient. For even now, despite her holiness, and her devotion to the Immaculate Mother of Christ, no one knew for certain whether or not Sister Catherine really was the Sister of the apparitions.

"My Sister," gently expostulated the young nun who had been indiscreet, "I was told in the Seminary that the Blessed Virgin appeared to the Sister in charge of the chicken yard at Enghien, and I believe it."

"But my little one," sweetly replied Sister Catherine, "know that it is very imprudent thus to speak at random!"

Not yet had her secret been revealed. Others might only surmise. In the meantime her mission had been successfully carried out, and as the greatest proof — if any further had been needed — of the admirable virtue of the humble

Daughter of Charity she continued to perform her lowly tasks in the kitchen and in the hospital, as portress, as caretaker of the chickens, and in all the least duties of a religious community.

As the decree of her beatification states, "the very humble employments which obedience confided to her, were filled by Catherine during her entire life, a life unknown to man; she preserved with care that simplicity and ardent charity which were recommended to her by the doctrine and precepts of her father, St. Vincent." Indeed hers was a hidden life, but a life hidden with Christ and His Mother in God, and hence one of untold fruitfulness for souls.

Catherine Labouré took her secret with her to the grave. She had served her Queen faithfully, she had done the work that had been given her to do and she continued unknown and unsung. God, however, and the Blessed Mother are not to be outdone in generosity. They have seen to it that the praises of their faithful servant are being sung today by great numbers of the faithful, and especially have they rewarded her with the reward exceeding great, eternal bliss with them forever in heaven. Catherine no longer need remember the visions of her Queen, for she now can look on her face to face in the presence of her King!

Catherine died a holy death on December 31, 1876. Not long after, the report of her sanctity spread abroad, and her secret was rightly divulged throughout the whole Christian world. She was beatified by His Holiness Pope Pius XI, in 1933. As the great Pontiff said of her:

"She knew how to keep the secret of her King, but above all, the secret of her Queen."

useless (Catherine's sharp wit could always find an answer), they got ready to leave. A few good-bys, a parting jest about old maids, a slam of the door, and Catherine was left alone in the *atrium*. A servant maid, a few years younger than Catherine, came in answer to the summons of her mistress.

"Agnes," Catherine said, "I am going to the emperor's palace! I'm going to ask him to let the Christians alone."

The city of Alexandria was in a turmoil. Maximinus II, emperor, had commanded all his subjects to make sacrifice to the pagan gods at a shrine in the central part of the metropolis. Christians, refusing to obey, were tempted to apostatize by promises, threats, and physical torture. If one had been in Alexandria at that time, he could have seen large droves of cattle, sheep, and goats being driven to the city from the countryside to be sold at the market place as sacrificial offerings. From morning till night the air was filled with bellowings and bleatings, with the sharp cries and curses of the drovers, the petulant hagglings of the buyers and sellers. The atmosphere itself became stifling with the mingled odors of beasts and the sweating bodies of men. Everywhere there were shouts and screams, laughter and crying.

Catherine was an only child. From her infancy she had been the tender object of care of her parents, but in spite of this fact she had remained unsophisticated and unspoiled. Sweetness radiated from her wherever she went, and all she met were charmed by her attractive personality. To these personal endowments were added intellectual accomplishments of the highest order. Her native wit and an analytic mind were sharpened and deepened by the best scholars of the day. Patience, long drilling, and hard work had brought her to that eminence which we call brilliance.

Like most of the sons and daughters of the wealthy in the early part of the fourth century, Catherine had led a rather carefree, unconcerned life. After the completion of their daily schooling the youth of that day turned their thoughts automatically to the delights of the palaestra, the theater, and the pleasure of company. Not that they were not good Christians. On the contrary, Catherine was a very good girl. But things which happened outside her restricted sphere of life concerned her very little.

And so, the sight she had experienced on the street outside her home had struck her very forcibly. It woke her up, so to speak, to another world. It lifted her out of her circumscribed existence and gave her a broader view of life. She felt a desire to help those poor unfortunates and her mind was restless until she resolved to see the emperor.

Catherine, together with her maid, elbowed her way through the noisy crowd to the palace of the apotheosized ruler. She was admitted to the audience chamber where she found the emperor seated in a black-lacquered, gold-inlaid throne, surrounded by a number of richly dressed lords and ladies. On seeing her, the emperor graciously waved, bidding her approach. Her obeisance made, she ignored the courtiers and the ladies, and immediately spoke her mind about the emperor's persecution of the Christians. As she progressed in her denouncement of his cruelty and barbarity, she grew more and more heated.

The emperor and his court were astounded. That a chit

of a girl would dare to front this half-god and upbraid him was almost unbelievable! At first Maximinus was furious, but as he listened to the flow of language his rage began to turn to admiration.

When she had finished speaking, the emperor began to reason with her, but in this intellectual combat he proved to be very much her inferior. You see, Catherine was endowed with extraordinary talents. She was a philosopher, a linguist, and was versed in many of the physical sciences. Not even reputed philosophers and barristers were her equal, and Maximinus, while an educated man, was no offspring of the god of the silver bow. But did you ever hear of an emperor set at naught? Emperors have more than just a solitary ace up their sleeve.

In this case he issued a mandate requiring the most brilliant scholars — and in his dominion a scintillating galaxy was found — to come to the court and debate with the girl.

They came — fifty strong.

The day following their arrival Catherine was summoned to dispute with them. When they looked upon her for the first time they thought it was a joke — for how could a girl so young, so immature, stand against the skill of sophists? The most learned of the company, turning to the emperor, stated with braggadocio:

"If I don't put her to silence with my first words you can take my head."

Ah! the idle boasts of men! Her adversaries plied her with questions and arguments from Plato, Aristotle, and many a rhetorician, trying to shake her faith. They hurled sophistic objections, unscrewed syllogisms, cited quotations from leading authorities. The air was electrified by the tension and earnestness of the battle. All listened intently. There was hardly a point upon which Catherine's opponents did not touch, hardly a crevice in which they did not try to get a foothold, but to all she answered with clear, cogent reasoning, and even convicted them by their own arguments. At last, baffled, they acknowledged themselves beaten, and even professed belief in Catherine's religion!

Maximinus was infuriated. Pale with anger, he ordered a fire to be kindled and them to be thrown into it.

Realizing, however, that efforts to convince Catherine were unavailing, the despot attempted to win her with promises of glory, as Satan once tempted the Son of God.

"Now look here, my dear girl, if you will but sacrifice to the gods, and especially to the leader of the choir of the Muses to whom you owe all your wisdom, half my kingdom is yours, and what's more, I'll make you my queen."

But Catherine was worldly wise too. She knew that he already had a wife. And as for his promise — he had no more intention of giving her half the realm than of resigning his throne altogether.

"You're only wasting time and breath with such talk. I belong to Christ. Much more do I prefer the robe of virginity and of martyrdom to the purple robe of majesty."

"Don't force me against my will to injure that fine robe of yours!" he threatened.

"Do what you wish," she rejoined, "for I shall soon pass to the magnificent dwellings of heaven, and I shall take with me many others who believe in Christ."

Shaking with rage, the tyrant ordered her to be stripped and scourged. For a long time her delicate body was lacerated with whips, until streams of blood flowed copiously, the only evidence she gave that her flesh was not of stone. At length, convinced that she would never yield to the torture, the emperor ordered her to be taken to prison until he should consider what to do with her.

Augusta, the wife of Maximinus, was a gentle, sympathetic woman, and charitable to the poor. When she learned of the state of Catherine, she determined to visit her in her duress. To this end she called Porphyrion, the emperor's lieutenant, and late that night, they stole secretly out of the palace, disguised, and proceeded to the jail. There they spoke with the suffering girl, and such was the efficacy and power of her words that they both became Christians and publicly proclaimed themselves so to the emperor on the following day.

When his wife came before him and stated that she too believed in the God of Catherine, the ruler was so infuriated that he immediately ordered her to be beheaded. As she was being led away, Porphyrion came forward and with him two hundred soldiers who likewise professed Christianity.

"We also have become Christians," he stated, his voice ringing throughout the chamber. "We have joined the army of Christianity.

The emperor fell back in amazement crying, "Alas, even Porphyrion, the leader of my cohorts has deserted me! I shall die when I destroy the glorious Porphyrion."

That day Christ enrolled in His heavenly army two hundred brave fighting men and their fearless leader.

The emperor now turned his attention to the young girl who seemed to bring so much misfortune to him. He had prepared a diabolical machine consisting of wheels rotating horizontally underneath a huge drum. The wheels were accoutered with sharp, runcinated spikes, which would tear to pieces a body placed on the drum. Catherine was now brought forward and the torture indicated to her. A momentary gleam of fear flashed in her eyes, but she recovered herself quickly and said that she was prepared to give her life for her faith.

But when the tender maiden was lashed to the drum, either through some imperfection in the apparatus, or through divine intervention, the whole mechanism burst apart. After the flurry created by this accident had subsided, the emperor endeavored again to seduce her with caresses and promises. The girl was as stern in repulsing him as before.

When at last the despot realized that he was powerless to break or subdue her, he stood up, imperially flung back his toga, and pronounced the sentence of death. A last malevolent look upon the adamantine spirit before him, a savage oath, and he left the tribunal.

Breathing heavily, while her heart pounded furiously, Catherine stood there, the sentence dully echoing in her ears. Her arms, bound tightly to her sides as yet unhealed from the scourging, gave her much pain. Her disheveled hair straggled about her face and shoulders. Though she had not been allowed the comfort of washing herself and arranging her person for several days, her beauty was still remarkable. The guards came forward and she was led to the place of execution. There she begged a few minutes grace in which to prepare to die.

There is no human being that does not feel some fear at the approach of death. Catherine was human. She was at the doorstep of eternity, and a little qualm passed over her as she looked forward to the unknown. The past was behind her —

for that she had no thought save sorrow for her faults — but death, and after death? She needed to bolster up her courage, to conquer her natural fear. The reprieve was granted by the rough executioner, and while a crowd of sympathetic women stood round her weeping, she opened her pure soul to God.

"My Lord Jesus Christ, I give Thee thanks, because Thou hast strengthened and guided me. Now I beg Thee to extend Thy arms, wounded on the cross for me, and receive my spirit, which I now sacrifice in confessing Thee. Remember Lord, that I am only flesh and blood; permit not that the things I did in my youth and in my ignorance may be counted against me at Thy Sacred Tribunal. Let my sins be blotted out by my blood. Look graciously, Lord, on this people standing here, and lead them by the light of Thy knowledge. Grant to them also, who may ask of Thee in my name, the things which they ask, provided they be conducive to their good; that Thy name may be praised forever."

She finished her prayer during which her pale, drawn face had become flushed, and a more brilliant beauty suffused her whole countenance. Calmly she turned her glowing, lustrous eyes to the executioner and bade him perform the task enjoined him. The old soldier's hand quivered for an instant as the girl put her head into place. The sword was raised, reached the peak, paused, descended. And Catherine's unstained soul went swiftly, as with the wings of angels, to the side of the King of kings.

This, then, is the story of St. Catherine of Alexandria, simple in substance and simply told. There is no one who will not love this girl, so tender and lovable, so modern, so human, and yet withal so saintly.

13

The Maid that Conquered

LUCY

HISTORY has often left us little more than a few salient and essential facts in the lives of the early martyrs. Yet their illustrious names have continued through the centuries in the unbroken veneration of the faithful and remain enshrined today in the minds and hearts of all the Church's children. Endeared to us by such a memory is the name of St. Lucy.

History records of her, with reasonable certainty, the date and place of her martyrdom. We know that she bravely offered up her life for Christ about the year 304, at Syracuse, in Sicily, during the persecution of Diocletian. Legend and folklore richly supply the rest. We shall here attempt to tell in all its simplicity and beauty the story as it has been told innumerable times and is written in ancient volumes.

At Syracuse, in Sicily, about the year 283, Lucy was born of parents noted alike for wealth and nobility of rank. Her father died when she was still in her early childhood. The entire care for the child, therefore, devolved upon the mother, Eutychia, who religiously brought up the lively little girl that later was to show such strength of faith and power of character.

Like so many of the early martyrs, Lucy in her young

maidenhood vowed her virginity to God. To Him she wished still further to devote herself entirely by proposing to distribute all her worldly goods to the poor. Her mother did not as yet approve of all this, but before long her judgment was to undergo a great change.

The city of Catania, legends tell us, was famous at this time for holding within its walls the hallowed remains of St. Agatha, the Virgin Martyr. Thousands of pilgrims flocked to her sepulcher. This inspired in Lucy the thought of visiting that shrine to obtain a special favor. Her mother, namely, had for years been afflicted with hemorrhage, which was sure to bring about in course of time serious consequences. Why not go with her then to the tomb of the great Virgin Martyr and there pray for relief in this distressful malady? The proposal pleased Eutychia, and together, mother and daughter set out upon their pilgrimage, light of heart and high in hope.

As Providence disposed, the two women arrived at Catania just as the ceremonies were being held in honor of the Saint, and they there heard read to them the very passage of the Gospel which relates the story of the woman who suffered from a flow of blood, and on touching the hem of our Lord's garment was healed immediately. Whereupon Lucy exclaimed to her mother:

"Oh, Mother, if you believe in this gospel story, believe that St. Agatha suffered for Christ and merited to have Him forever in her presence for whom she died. Step up and touch the sepulcher, then, and your faith will obtain relief for you."

So when the throng had gradually departed from the tomb,

mother and daughter together prostrated themselves before the image of the Saint, and with tears besought her aid. While they were thus praying, a vision appeared to Lucy. She saw St. Agatha standing radiant amid a multitude of angels, and heard her ask:

"My sister Lucy, what is it you wish of me? Do you ask your mother's cure? Well, your faith has strengthened the faith of your mother. Behold, she is wholly cured. I also tell you now that just as Christ has exalted the city of Catania through me, so He will honor Syracuse through you, because you have prepared a pleasing dwelling place for Christ in your chaste heart."

When Lucy heard these words she arose, trembling with excitement, and embraced her mother, saying:

"Mother, mother dear, at last you are really cured!" Then in a more subdued tone, "And I ask you, mother, in view of St. Agatha's prophecy to me, not to expect me to marry. I wish to give myself and everything I have to Christ."

A changed Eutychia replied, "Yes, Lucy, you may do as you desire with your inheritance, and I will add the greater portion of my own fortune to your offering."

Thus the mother and daughter were made one in Christ, both in thought and desire. They forthwith began to distribute their wealth among the poor and the needy. But such a gesture was not destined to be passed by unnoticed. News of their largess came to the notice of Lucy's betrothed and stirred his greed beyond control. In a fit of anger, he denounced her to the governor, Paschasius, as a Christian.

Brought before the tribunal of the governor and interrogated by him, Lucy said:

"It is a sacrifice in the eyes of the living God to befriend widows and orphans in their tribulation. For three years, now, I have done nothing else. Since I have no worldly goods to sacrifice, I gladly offer myself as a living sacrifice to God."

To this Paschasius answered: "You can speak thus to every Christian like yourself, but before me, who keep the decrees of the emperor, you use such language in vain."

"You observe the laws of the emperor," Lucy replied. "I obey the laws of God. You fear the emperor; I fear God. You do not wish to offend the emperor; I take care not to offend God. You seek to please an earthly sovereign; my sole desire is to please God. You do whatever *seems* useful to you; I do what I *know* is good *and* useful."

Paschasius by this time was becoming exasperated, and in anger shouted: "You have squandered your fortune with wicked men, and you even talk like an evil woman."

"My fortune is now in good and deserving hands," quietly Lucy replied, "and I have never acted in any shameful way. You are corrupters of men's minds, of whom the Apostle says: 'Evil communications corrupt good manners.' For you persuade men to sin and to deny God."

"Stop, lest I strike you down!" cried Paschasius.

With the meekness of Christ before Caiphas Lucy answered, "You cannot stop the word of God."

"Are you God, then?" asked Paschasius sarcastically.

"No," retorted Lucy, "I am but a handmaid of God, and therefore I speak the word of God, for He has said: 'But when they shall deliver you up, take no thought how or what to speak: for it shall be given you in that hour what to speak; for it is not you that speak, but the spirit of your Father that speaketh in you.'"

At such an answer from a mere stripling of a girl, Paschasius ordered that Lucy should be sent to a place of sin, to which she calmly replied:

"My body will never be defiled without the consent of my own will. For even if you were to put incense into my hands, and force me to offer sacrifice, God would look with ridicule upon such an act. For it is God who judges our desires and actions. So even if you should have me defiled by force, it would but serve doubly to enrich my crown."

Paschasius countered, "I will see to it that you die in shame, unless you offer up a sacrifice to the Augusti."

To this threat of brute force Lucy undauntedly answered: "As I have already told you, you cannot force my will to consent to sin, and whatever you may do to my body, which you seem to have in your power, cannot in any way affect the handmaid of Christ."

Thinking to frighten her into submission, Paschasius then ordered that she be taken out of the court. Three rough-faced legionaries stepped up to lay their coarse hands on her. But she could not be moved from her place. By the power of God she seemed rooted to the spot. Ropes were passed around her body to drag her away, but still she remained immovable. Paschasius now was in a frenzy.

He summoned soothsayers and priests from the temple to exercise their rites on her; but all to no avail.

"Why is it," asked the governor, "that a frail little girl like you cannot be moved by a hundred men?"

To this Lucy confidently replied: "Were you to use ten thousand men, God would still protect me."

Paschasius had come to the end of his devices.

"Why are you troubled?" Lucy interposed. "Now that you

have visible proof that I am truly a temple of the Holy Ghost, believe in Him."

In more dire straits than ever, Paschasius ordered her person to be covered with pitch and oil and a huge fire built about her. But, as before, Lucy remained totally unharmed. Standing in the midst of the flames she spoke calmly and courageously addressing Paschasius and his court:

"I have asked my Lord, Jesus Christ, that this fire might not overcome me, and thus my martyrdom might be delayed, in order that I might remove any fear of suffering from those who believe in Christ, and that I might confound you and all unbelievers."

In a towering rage, Paschasius commanded, as a last resort, that Lucy should be put to the sword. But even when the steel had pierced her, she spoke out in a clear, triumphant tone, and her voice was as the sound of a trumpet proclaiming victory.

"I announce to you great tidings," she exclaimed, "peace has returned to the Church of God. Diocletian has been deposed and Maximian has died this very day. And know that just as the people of Catania have my sister Agatha for their intercessor in heaven, so God in His goodness has given me to this city of yours to intercede for you. Be of good hope and obey in all things the Will of God."

With these words on her lips, Lucy rendered up her valiant soul into the hands of her Maker. She had offered her life as a sacrifice, and He has accepted it. Triumphantly she went to enjoy her eternal reward in the company of those countless virgins who "follow the Lamb whithersoever He goeth."

14

The Lily of the Mohawks
KATERI TEKAKWITHA

ARESKOI, the Sun, seemed to leap with unwonted haste along the blue-green pathways of the treetops, threatening to plunge at any moment into the red-gold sea that lay beyond the purple-misted shoulders of the valley of the Mohawk. Behind him streamed his ruddy hair, flashing all the colors of the wampum belt. On his heels there ran the night in her long transparent twilight veil of purple gray.

The little finch and sparrow were making for their well-woven homes in the branches of the forest. The busy squirrel and rabbit, impatient to be in their lodges with the young ones, scampered through the umber thorns and green-red bushes of wild berries. There was the soft dull rustle of maple leaves that stir in the last day breezes.

It was evening, the dying time of day, and with it came that peace that a mighty warrior feels as he breathes his last, full knowing that his life has been well spent.

From her little mat of beaver skins, just inside the longhouse door, an Indian maid sat looking and listening, for she loved all these things. A long while she watched Areskoi in his race. She saw him skim the rocky hills, then leap across the sky from tree to tree, she thought, like a hunter, like her uncle when he jumped across the little brook there by the edge of the village field.

Oh, of course, she knew *now* that Areskoi really was not a living person, much less the god she once had thought him. But surely Rawenniio, the true God of the Christians, would not mind if she, so very much an Iroquois, still liked to sit and imagine that she saw the great red orb take the form of a mighty bowman who stalked across the blue-gray sky in search of beaver and of elk. Had not Father de Lamberville told her of a great sachem of the Christians who long ago had called the sun his brother and the earth his mother? a saint who preached to fishes and spoke to birds and wolves? She thought that she would like to have met and talked with Francis who could see God in the burnt-brown autumn leaves and the smiling skies of summer. She would tell him how long before she had become a Christian she used to speak to Rawenniio in the forests where she felt she saw Him everywhere, how she loved and promised to always love Him even though she was not quite sure just who He was.

See how the shadows of the lodge poles fall upon the mat-strewn floor, like the long-stemmed, broad-bowled calumets of the elders of the tribe! And there, the center beam stands in the graying cabin light like — why she had never noticed that before! — it stands joined to the roof support like the little cross on the chapel door, like the cross that Ondessonk, the Blackrobe Father Jogues, had carved on the bark of birch trees in the forests of the Mohawk.

Almost instinctively her nimble fingers, which had been busily sewing together the red and blue and bright green porcupine-quill trimmings for her aunt's new deer-skin jacket, paused. Then slowly and very reverently she made the sign of the cross, the sign which had meant the death of

René Goupil, Ondessonk's best friend, the sign that made her so disliked by the pagans in the village.

"In the name of the Father, and of the Son, and of the Holy Ghost. Amen."

Why did the people of her clan and of her castle hate that sign so much? If they only knew what it meant, she was sure they would love it as much as she did. For a moment she clasped her hands in a silent little prayer that Rawenniio would make all her Iroquois, especially her village of Gandaowagué, Christians, good and true. Then suddenly she turned. There was a soft crunching of leaves outside the cabin door. Could it be her aunt back from the fields so soon? She saw a long dark hand lift up the bearskin flap that covered the lodge opening, and a brave stepped in. It was Wild Eagle.

In the red indistinct light of the setting sun she saw his bronzed face twisted into a most hideous sneer. The muscles of his face quivered with anger, his teeth were clenched in grinding hate, his eyes were black with death. Cautiously he stepped across the log threshold, then dropped the flap over the opening of the door. He paused just a moment, spat through his snarling lips, then slowly drew his long-handled, broad-bladed hatchet from his belt. Deliberately, like a wolf stalking a young deer, he came across the floor until he stood towering above the Indian maiden. Slowly he raised his tomahawk. His face convulsed. His body shook with anger.

"Tekakwitha, I hate you. Once I offered to marry you. I came to your uncle's lodge to eat the bowl of sagamité. You ran away. I felt the insult. I hated you then, Tekakwitha, and would have killed you long ago if it had not been for your uncle. Now you are a Christian. I hate Christians. Now

I hate you more. I just saw you make that magic sign of the Blackrobes and the Christians. That sign is bad luck. That sign I hate more than anything. I am going to do to you what our brothers the Bear clan did to the friend of Ondessonk for making that sign unless you give up all this foolishness. You are an Iroquois. Iroquois should not be Christians."

"Wild Eagle, you cannot frighten me. Do you think that just because you threaten me I will quit being a Christian? I could ask for nothing more than to die, to be tomahawked, because I believe in Rawenniio. Strike, Wild Eagle, strike! Make me a martyr like the Blackrobes Breboeuf and Chabenel, and like my namesake Catherine."

The hatchet in the red hand swung back, then — then Wild Eagle hesitated. He looked down at Tekakwitha kneeling on her mat with calm, half-smiling eyes. His arm relaxed. The tomahawk fell to the ground. A strange sense of fear erased the anger from his face. He dropped his eyes, muttered some half-intelligible words, turned and rushed out of the cabin. For just a moment Tekakwitha watched the bearskin flap still shaking from Wild Eagle's hurried exit. Then, smiling to herself and shaking her head, she turned and gathered together her bone needles, rough thread, and colored quills. She packed them in the little beaver sewing bag and hung it from a lodge pole. She would have to hurry now if she would have the fire ready and the food warm when her aunt and her uncle came back.

As she alternately fanned the little blaze and wiped the smoke tears from her eyes, Tekakwitha, or Kateri as she liked to be called (for that was her Christian name, given to her by Father de Lamberville because Catherine of Alexandria, the virgin martyr, had been a great lover of the Trinity and hated all false gods), went back over the not so very long story of her life.

Tegonhatsihongo, Anastasia, as she now was named, had often told Kateri of her early summers. Kateri's mother had been an Algonquin Christian who had been captured in a Mohawk raid and brought back to be the wife of the Turtle chief, her father. Her mother had never forgotten Rawenniio, and spoke often of Him to the other Indian women. When Kateri was born (1656) her mother had planned to have her baptized by the Blackrobes, but war between the French and the Five Nations had prevented the Jesuit Fathers from coming to Ossernonon. Hardly four winters had passed (1660) when the scourge of smallpox swept over the lodges of the Mohawks. In that dreadful dark day her father, mother, and little brother had been carried off. She herself had been close to death and even now, in her pock-marked face and weakened eyes, were borne the signs of the dread disease. With her father's death, Kateri's uncle became chief of the Turtles and adopted her into his lodge.

The castle at Ossernonon had been burned lest the contagion break out anew, and a new home was built at Gandaowagué. Here Tekakwitha grew into a real Iroquois maiden with her shiny black, braided hair, deer-skin dress, and beaded moccasins. Here she learned how to cook the beaver and the elk, to sew, to fashion wooden bowls, to plant and reap, to build bark lodges, and the thousand other things. Here she heard the stories of the cruel Areskoi, god of war, and of Thohoroniawagon, the overlord of hunting and of fishing, and of the hero Hiawatha. And here she had begun to feel that first strange yearning for the One she called Rawenniio.

There had been happy times, of feasting, of hunting, and of harvesting. And there had been sad ones, too. Tekakwitha had seen ten plantings come and go (1666) when the French with their great thundersticks and fire had swept the valley and burned her home. She remembered the confusion in the village as the sachems in solemn council plunged the point of the ax into the earth and gave the order that all were to move to Thionnontogen and leave Gandaowagué of the Turtles and Andagoron of the Bears undefended. She had helped her aunt gather all their food and household things, and carried them in many journeys to the triple-palisaded castle of the Wolves.

She could still see the fire in the village square at which her uncle and the Mohawks burned their captives in propitiation to Areskoi. Tekakwitha had not watched that sickening sacrifice. Though an Iroquois through and through she could never bear to see the cruelties of her relatives, spent on the helpless victims of their raids. Instead, this time, she ran up to the platform around the palisaded wall and looked out across the rolling hills toward the north and east from which the French would come.

Suddenly a flame shot up behind the far line of hemlocks and of oaks. The French had reached Gandaowagué. Her long house was being burned. She turned and shouted as loudly as she could. The braves and squaws around the sacrificial fire paused, then more vigorously than ever they began to dance and sing and prod the captives with lighted brands. Another twisting tongue of flame sprang up, this time a little more toward the east. Andagoron was burning. She watched. Along the trail from the burning Mohawk castles the few warriors who had stayed until the end, came racing with news that De Tracy and his men were coming on to Thionnontogen. The place was in an uproar. Tekakwitha's uncle gave orders for all the women, children, and old men to fly into the forest and hide. The warriors were to stay and defend the lodges.

Slowly the French came across the level ground that lay before the walls of the village. They stopped. Bluecoated soldiers swung two iron cannons into position. A match flared. A roar shook the valley. The Mohawk braves, with one accord, threw down their arms and raced for the woods. Soon the long houses of Thionnontogen were crackling in the flames.

The defeat of the Iroquois by De Tracy, though won more by the fear engendered by his cannon than by actual combat, broke for a time the resistance of the Five Nations. A treaty was made between the two parties, an opportunity was given to the Blackrobes to go once more among the beloved savages of Jogues and Goupil.

The last birchbark sheets of the long house had scarcely been sewn together in the new castle of Gandaowagué when three Fathers of the Society of Jesus came to visit Tekakwitha's lodge. They were Père Frémin, Père Bruyas, and Père Pierron who were on their way to the new village of the Wolves at Thionnontogen. While they stayed in her uncle's long house, Tekakwitha served them and listened to everything they had to say. She marveled at the wonderful ways in which the Father could explain the movements of the stars, the habits of the animals, the reasons for the summer and the snows. She listened with all the curiosity of a simple Indian maid to the stories of the power of the governor of the French, Onontiio, so the Iroquois called him, and the splendor of the Great Chief across the Big Waters in France. But most of all she loved to hear Père Frémin tell of Rawenniio, who suffered and died that all might live, that all Indians, hated Huron and Iroquois, might go to a heaven where all worldly cares would be forgotten. There in the heaven of Rawenniio there would be no burning captives nor enemy whose bloody hatchet sought to cleave one's head. There would be no famine and no thirst, for the corn would stand ripened all the year and the streams would never freeze. There everyone could have anything he wanted. But, best of all, Rawenniio would be there to sit around the fire while the kettle swung, and He would tell them everlasting stories while the sachems smoked the calumet.

When the Blackrobes left for Thionnontogen many of the Turtles accompanied them in order to be present at the reception. It was there the Fathers established the mission of St. Mary's and built a little bark chapel. Soon afterwards Père Bruyas took the hunting trail westward to the Oneidas and Père Pierron went to the Iroquois cabins toward the rising sun. A few summers later (1668) Père Pierron passed through the Turtle castle on his way back from Quebec to St. Mary's where he took charge.

About this time the war cry was raised against the Mohicans and for the rest of the summer the Mohawks of Gandaowagué and Thionnontogen were either on the war trail or busily defending their lodges. Père Pierron was kept quite busy with the injured and the sick of both enemy and friend. The uncertainty that hung over every trail, the ever-present danger that a Loup lurked behind each forest bush and tree, the danger that a raiding party might swoop at any moment on the village, all made the Indians more attentive to the Blackrobe's words.

Conversions were becoming a bit more numerous. Vice, especially drunkenness, was becoming a bit more uncommon. For this last the Mohawk chiefs were grateful to the Fathers. Ever since the fur traders of New York, Albany, and Quebec had given whiskey as barter for pelts, the tribes and clans had suffered. Men and women, young and old, would revel in drunken riots for days on end. The braves were weakened and no longer the Men above Others, Onkwe Onwe. The young men were more unruly and listened less to the counsel of their elders. Theft, murder, and a hundred other things were breaking the morale of the Five Nations. The chiefs shook their heads in sad lament. Something must be done. And then the Blackrobes came. They saw to it, as best they could, that the French traders were forbidden to give the savages the firewater that made them demons. They sent a petition to the Governor-General of Manhattan who promised his cooperation. Though far from satisfactory, the progress in the drive to clean up the public morals was a consolation to both the Fathers and the sachems. It made them better men, more disposed to listen to the words of the Jesuits, and it made them better warriors, more fit to drive off the now very dangerous Mohicans.

During these years of incessant warfare, Tekakwitha and her relatives moved to a new castle at Caughnawaga. It was here that she grew into young womanhood. It was here that she had prepared the gifts for the dead in the great burial ceremony. It was within those very bark walls that she had come to the decision not to marry and had spurned Wild Eagle's proposal. It was at Caughnawaga that she first met Father de Lamberville who made her a Christian.

It seemed as though it were but one sun ago that she had been sitting on her lodge seat sewing when the missionary entered the cabin of her uncle. She had cut her foot on a fallen tree and had to stay at home rather than go into the fields to hoe the maize. So she took out her little beaver bag and began to weave her colored beads into a new design for the cover of her uncle's quiver. She had been so intent upon her work that she had not noticed the Father in the doorway. When he finally called her name she turned startled. Then, seeing who it was, she asked him to come in. They had a friendly little chat. She explained the bead design and showed him how to thread and work the needle. He told her a few little stories about Quebec and France, and then about Rawenniio. Impulsively, she still did not know why, she had breathlessly told the Father that she wanted, oh, so badly, to be a Christian.

At first Father de Lamberville seemed very much surprised. She rushed on with her story. She told him how she had been able to see Rawenniio in every leaf and stone. She told him of her mother and her Christian life. She begged him with tears in her eyes to give her the Prayer. The missionary hesitated. Tekakwitha was the niece of the great chief, the enemy of the Christians. Her aunts were among the most bitter contemners of the new converts. No, she would have to wait. This was a matter of much calm deliberation. Tekakwitha pleaded. If she did not become a Christian she would die. Her heart would break. She did not care what anyone thought. She would be glad to be jeered at and scolded by her aunts. Her uncle's anger would not make her change her mind. If she could become a Christian she would never, never deny Rawenniio. She would go through four, or five, or six times the tortures of Fathers Jogues and Breboeuf. Would not Père de Lamberville hear her prayer?

The Blackrobe was won over. He consented to instruct her, even though it might bring down upon them both her uncle's wrath. But, strange to say, the chief was not mad. Perhaps he thought it a wiser course to permit Tekakwitha to become a Christian and thus keep her in the lodge rather than refuse and give her cause to run away to the new Praying Castle at Caughnawaga in Canada.

Whenever the chief thought of this new mission of the Blackrobes his eyes grew dark with anger. Were they not taking from him many of his best hunters and braves? Had not Kryn, the "great Mohawk," conqueror of the Mohicans, renounced his village and gone there to live? Kryn, Togouiroui, who now called himself Joseph, had once been the greatest fighter of the Five Nation's long houses. Whenever the hatchet was raised and the war paint put on Kryn was chosen to lead the assault. No Mohawk, bravest of the brave, could equal him in valor on the field. No one could shoot as steadily. No one could stalk as quietly. No one could swing the bloody tomahawk with half the skill and strength of the "Mohawk of the Mohawks." But now he was a Christian, one who no longer believed in Areskoi, and dreams of manitous, or got drunk and had many wives. These things were forbidden in the new Caughnawaga.

It had all started when Kryn's wife became a Christian. That had been bad luck, so Tekakwitha's uncle thought. Once she had received the Prayer she never ceased to prod and coax her husband to do the same. Kryn at first was furious. Then gradually he relented. He even went so far as to visit the Praying Castle at La Prairie. There he met Père Frémin. The chief was impressed by the orderliness and stability of the little mission. He came again, and then again, and stayed longer every time. Finally, one day in early autumn, he asked the Father to keep him and make him a Christian. He promised to be faithful and sincere. And he was.

It was not long before Kryn was accepted as the leader of the little Christian castle. His great reputation and natural powers of command made him one to be respected. Besides he poured all of his marvelous energy into his new vocation. He was not one to do things by halves. He constituted himself a sort of chief of police and saw to the discipline of the community. It was he who devised a very novel and most effective punishment for drunkards. He threw them in the sty with the hogs. If they managed to stagger to their feet and slip across the fence, he threw them right back until they were completely sober. In a very short time the flow of firewater was diminished no little.

All these things had been talked about around the lodge fires of the Iroquois. Many, even from Tekakwitha's castle, had gone to join Kryn. Many others, some of the best men of the tribe were on the point of going north. Had not even Hot Ashes gone into the mission? Hot Ashes, every bit as fiery as his name, and almost as brave and fierce as Kryn himself, had become a follower of the Blackrobes.

One day in that time of the year when Areskoi ran so close along the treetops that his flaming moccasins scorched the leaves and burnt them brown, Hot Ashes set out all alone on the warpath. A relative of his had been slain, by the French, someone had told him. He planned to get revenge. Along the forest trails that led northward to Montreal he sped with black hatred in his heart. All alone he would swing the hatchet and wet his knife with blood. Perhaps he would be killed by the thundersticks of the French, but not before he had counted many coups, not before he had taken many scalps.

As he followed the twisting mountain trail that brought him to the great waters of the St. Lawrence, he was overtaken by a runner from his clan who told him, just in time, that the French had not killed his brother. The murder had been done by Indians of a western tribe. Hot Ashes camped that night on the slate gray bluffs where the rocks seemed to crumble and plunge into the white soapy rapids of the great river. He had to take counsel with himself. What should be his next move? If he went home he would have to take up the war club and the peace between his people and the French would be broken. He was running short of food, and he had not many arrows left. Perhaps it would be better to go on to the French mission of St. Francis Xavier du Sault. At least it would be interesting to see how the Christians lived. Hot Ashes went and stayed. Like Kryn, a man who never left things undone, he became chief of his people there, the Oneidas. As a matter of fact, he even rose higher than Kryn, the Grand Agnié, as he was chief of the dogiques, the spiritual monitors of the Christian Indians. But even more than this was his desire. He wanted to be a real missionary, to return and evangelize his people. And he would do so.

All these things, too, had been discussed in the councils of the Five Nations. Tekakwitha's uncle had often expressed his contempt for the once great Kryn and Hot Ashes. In his eyes they were renegades far beneath his notice. How differently he would have thought had he known what one of these Christian braves was going to do to him not so very far in the future. How he would have hated him!

But now that Tekakwitha came with her insistent pleas to be baptized the old chief thought it best to give in. She would soon forget all about the Prayer. And it might be worth while humoring her just to prevent any wild ideas of joining the Christians at the Sault. As long as he could keep her in his castle he was sure to have her help. Soon, too, she would have to marry, and that would mean another bow in the lodge and more venison for the kettle. Yes, it would be wiser to let her have her way.

Père de Lamberville was agreeably surprised by the intelligence and earnestness of his neophyte. The little Indian maiden learned her prayers and the necessary doctrines of the Christian faith with such rapidity and certainty that the Jesuit promised to baptize her on the coming Easter Sunday (1676).

Tekakwitha, of course, could hardly wait until that joyous morning. When it came the little chapel was gaily decorated with ferns, and flowers, and the sweet-smelling branches of the pine, and crowded with all the people of the castle in their brightest robes and blankets. The ceremony was simple but very solemn. To the Indians, both pagan and Christian, it meant a great deal. The daughter of their chief was receiving the Prayer. Tekakwitha, the brightest flower of the pagan bark long houses, was now Kateri, the Lily of the Mohawks.

Everyone seemed to catch the spirit that animated the new convert. Everyone called her *the* Christian. Some meant it as an honor, others as contempt. And not least among these latter were her own aunts. They did everything, out of jealousy and hatred, to make life miserable for Kateri. They scolded and cursed her. They made her do much more than her share of the work in the lodge. They even went so far as to accuse her of a dreadful sin simply because she had forgotten a bit of Indian etiquette and called her uncle by his first name. They chided her for her constant refusal to attend the sacrificial burning of captives. They called her selfish, slothful, proud. When she refused Wild Eagle's proposal of marriage their anger knew no bounds. Every day and all day long Kateri was lashed by their sharp tongues. But she always managed to keep her same little smile. She tried to make her aunts like her. Although she was doing far more than her share of the work, she stayed yet longer in the fields, spent much more time over the steaming kettles, and sewed and trimmed the beaver robes that her uncle would trade to the Dutch. But it was no use. Her aunts would not relent.

Things had been going from bad to worse, thought Kateri, as she went one evening to the little spring beyond the palisades to fetch water for the sagamité she must prepare for supper. After she had filled her wooden bowl from the clear, cold spring, she paused a moment to watch the waters of the Mohawk splash and foam against the rocky shore. The last faint crimson rays of the setting sun flecked the white-capped little waves that swished against the banks. The hemlocks in the distance had lost their color and stood black outlined against the golden sky. As she gazed up the river she thought she saw something shoot around the nearest bend. It was something! She strained her poor weak eyes. It was a canoe with three men! For a moment she hesitated. Could it be Mohicans? Should she run and warn the village? But before she could quite make up her mind the canoe scraped against the bank. The men jumped out and pulled it up out of the water. Crouching behind a clump of forest bush, Kateri saw them hide their boat and then start along the trail to the village. Then she saw who they were. It was Hot Ashes, and her own brother-in-law, and a strange Huron. With a cry, half of welcome, half of relief, she pushed her way through the undergrowth to meet them.

"Hot Ashes! My brother-in-law!"

"Kateri! This is the best of luck!"

"What are you doing here?"

"We have come to get you and bring you to our mission."

"What? Me? To your mission? I don't understand."

"Well, little one, my wife, your adopted sister, has long urged me to come and free you from all this trial and sorrow. Hot Ashes and our friend here have kindly offered to help. But we must work quickly. Is your uncle in the castle?"

"No. He has gone to trade with the Dutch. I don't know when he will be back."

"That is good. We will have no trouble. Will you come?"

"Well, I . . ."

"Think well, my little sister, what we offer you."

"All right! When?"

"Tonight. You will take Hot Ashes' place in the canoe. Come. Let us go into the village."

Kateri could hardly wait until the night. Her heart beat so loudly she was afraid her aunts would hear and wonder why. She tried her best to do everything as ordinary as possible. But it was hard to keep her voice from trembling as she talked and her hand from shaking as she helped her aunt stir the kettle. But at last the dark did come. Kateri waited until everyone was sound asleep. Then, having quietly packed her little beaver bag with a bit of corn and a few sewing things, she lifted the bear-skin flap and stepped into the pitch blackness of the forest. She ran as fast as she could along the path that led to the river lest she should keep her friends waiting too long. But they were there. She took her place in the canoe. The men paddled it into the deeper waters and then with slow and steady rhythm drove it through the little waves.

For several days all went well. One morning, though, as Kateri and her brother-in-law were gathering wood for the campfire a shot rang out! It was the signal they had agreed upon should her uncle catch up with them. Kateri dove behind a fallen log and pulled handfuls of dry leaves over herself. If her uncle caught her it would be too bad for all of them. Fortunately, the Huron from Lorette was a good actor and managed to throw him off the trail by pretending that he was all alone and had fired at a passing bird and missed. The uncle went back thinking that he had wasted all of his time on a wild-goose chase. Kateri was safe now and need worry of no more interference.

From the Mohawk, through the Lake of the Blessed Sacrament, across Lake Champlain, along the River Richelieu to Chambly they journeyed. From here they went by forest trail to the mission of the Blackrobes.

When Kateri arrived at the Christian castle of Caughnawaga (1677) she was taken into the lodge of her old friend

Anastasia Tegonhatsihongo. She had brought with her a letter from Father de Lamberville to Father Cholenec in which her black-gowned friend told his brother Jesuit of the treasure he was sending, a real saint. Père Cholenec, however, was not one to jump at conclusions. He had been on the missions for a good number of years and knew the Indian temperament and character. They were fickle, unreliable, in some cases, and at least worthy of a general slight distrust. If this Mohawk maiden was a saint, she would have to prove it to him. And she did.

As she had been known as *the* Christian in Caughnawaga along the Mohawk, so she soon became known as *the* Christian in Caughnawaga along the St. Lawrence. So rapid was her progress that Father Cholenec decided to permit her to receive her First Holy Communion on Christmas (1677), less than a year after her arrival at the mission, a thing unheard of before. Kateri's reverence in the chapel, her modesty, humility, charity, patience, and obvious desire of perfection decided the pastor. For Kateri that Christmas was the happiest day of her life. From then on her progress along the road of sanctification became more and more evident.

Because she was so very much a child of the forests and a true daughter of the Iroquois, she could inflict upon herself such fierce penances that the Fathers had to command her to stop them. She slept on thorns, touched burning coals to her tender skin, and walked through the winter snows without her moccasins. Because she was so much a Christian, she could endure the calumnies and lies of her own friends and people. She had to undergo many of the same trials she had met in her old pagan home. A jealous wife accused her, falsely, of a very grave sin. Her kin made the same complaint of selfishness and pride because she refused to marry. But Kateri with her cheery smile never drew back from her ideal.

At the mission she met Marie Thérèse Tegaiaguenta, who was to become her best Christian friend. Thérèse was a sort of Iroquois Magdalen. Her chief claim to fame, or to notoriety, when she was still in the lodges of her people, had been her propensity to drink. She was one of the worst of a very bad set of weak-moraled pagans. Even after her baptism she had fallen again and again below even the standards of the pagans. But she was brought to her senses by a very disastrous hunting trip on which several of the party died mysteriously and she herself almost succumbed to the cannibalistic intentions of the rest. She came to the Sault and led a quite exemplary life. Since Kateri was obviously striving for the same heights of sanctity Thérèse was drawn to *the* Christian. Together they practiced severe penances. They formed a little mutual compact of prayer. They even planned to start an Iroquois sisterhood in imitation of the French nuns. And when Kateri (March 25, 1679) made her long-cherished vow of perpetual virginity it was Thérèse who made up for the abuse she had received from even her closest relations. The two were in all things inseparable.

Kateri did not live long after she arrived at Caughnawaga in Canada. In the blazing fire of her own zeal and desire of holiness, weakened by great penances, and afflicted by a serious disease, the Lily wilted rapidly. When at last she could go no longer into the fields to sow and reap, or follow on the trail to mend nets and broken traps, Kateri tried to keep on working from her sickbed. She had the women of the village bring their children to her lodge and there, lying on her little mat of skins, she would tell them stories. Stories of the forests, of the beaver, and of the elk. Stories of the warpath, of Kryn, and of Hiawatha. And stories of the great good God, Rawenniio, whom Father Cholenec talked to them about.

She grew weaker and weaker. At last, during Holy Week (1680), it was apparent that the end of the trail had been reached. On Wednesday (April 17), Thérèse was summoned from the fields to Kateri's side. This was the sign that all was just about over. For Kateri had told her friend that she would call her when she felt she was going to die.

For the last time the two friends prayed together, one the spotless Lily of the fields, the other the mottled tiger Lily. Then Thérèse bent down and kissed her fevered lips. Kateri smiled just a little, then with the words, "I will love you in heaven," she bade her last farewell to Marie Thérèse and all her friends. *The* Christian of Caughnawaga, the little Saint of the Sault, had left the castle of her people and was hastening, far faster than Areskoi in the time of the deep snows, along the golden trail that led through the gray-blue skies and snow-white clouds to the eternal council fire of Rawenniio. There forever and forever she could talk with Him, and look at Him, and love Him.

15

The Little Flower of Carmel
THÉRÈSE OF THE CHILD JESUS

As HE walked across the thick blue rugs to the entrance of her bedroom, he noticed how the sun, coming through the rose windows, played upon the myriad particles that filled the air in the hallway. He wondered if she would be ready to go in a few moments. He glanced into her room; suddenly his glance became fixed; he felt the rims of his eyes beginning to burn; and before he could ask her if she were ready, a lump rose into his throat.

She had never worn her hair like that before. She had always let the curls hang freely over her shoulder with only a ribbon to hold them in place. And now that M. Martin saw his daughter Thérèse with her hair braided, wrapped tightly around her head, and fastened into a large knot with a comb, he could not help thinking of the day thirty years ago that he had met a beautiful young girl just like Thérèse. Thirty years of memories of a happy married life overwhelmed him; and he looked all the more lovingly on Thérèse when he realized that the other was no more. Yet how alike they both were; he looked at his "little queen" as she arranged with slender fingers her fair hair. Yes, like her mother's, her hair had a glint of gold; her eyes, too, now busily intent upon a loose strand, were blue. (How charmingly vexed she appeared, he thought, with that determined look on her finely drawn and regular features. Her mother, too, had had an expression as clear and candid as that, breathing an air of peace.)

M. Martin had not noticed till this moment that his *"little queen"* was no longer little. . . . But before he could continue his musings Thérèse caught sight of him in her mirror, quickly turned, and with her fingers still arranging the knot, asked with vibrant expectancy:

"Daddy, how do you like me like this?"

M. Martin smiled, swallowed, and avoided her eyes. Thérèse went gaily on:

"Do you think that the Bishop will think that I look old enough now that I have my hair put up? Maybe he will think I am older if I make my voice low!"

M. Martin could only kiss her on the forehead in substitution for a reassuring answer; and as he went down the hall stairs and out the front door to wait to drive with her to the Bishop's home, he could hear the subdued murmurs of Thérèse trying to make her voice "low."

M. Martin stepped into the carriage, tightened the reins of the pawing horses and half muttered, half thought to himself: "I knew she was determined to become a nun, but I did not know she was so set upon it as all this."

Just two weeks ago when he had been in the back yard Thérèse had come home from Benediction and found him gardening there. The shy way she had come to greet him told M. Martin that she had something on her mind. He suspected what it was; so pressing her cheek close to himself he greeted her:

"My little queen, what is the matter? Come on, let's walk while you tell me."

Although Thérèse, because of her tears, hardly managed to utter a "Daddy, the Carmel," M. Martin immediately knew that she too wanted to become a nun as were her older sisters Marie and Pauline. M. Martin did not see why she should be the one to cry, since he would miss her much more than she would miss him; however, as he had prayed for some time to be able to make this sacrifice he did not mention this to her. They continued to walk, and in a few moments Thérèse's tears dried up and her heart was soothed. After a time, approaching a low wall, M. Martin pointed to some little white flowers which were like miniature lilies. Carefully reaching out he plucked one, gave it to Thérèse and explained with what care the Lord made it bloom, and had preserved it untouched until that day. Thérèse understood the action, and read her own life story in the story of that little flower. She noted how, in pulling it, he was careful not to break its roots, as if it was destined yet to grow, in a more fertile soil, in the sweet valley of the convent of Carmel.

The horses gave a little lurch forward and M. Martin was jerked out of his reverie and saw his daughter coming down the flagstone steps to the gravel drive. At first she ran; then realizing that "after all, I am no longer a child," she slowed down to a very ladylike walk, graciously accepted her father's hand to get into the seat beside him, and off they drove. Out of the front drive they went, past the oak trees on their front lawn, past the wooden swing of their neighbor's, past the hunchback bridges with the violets growing in the damp beneath (Thérèse mused how often she had collected them for the Blessed Virgin's May altar), past the Cathedral, and they were out of the little town of

Lisieux, off on their way to see the bishop of Bayeux.

"Father!" The voice of Thérèse could faintly be heard over the horses' hoofs. "My beloved king! Isn't this exciting? I wonder what the bishop will be like. Do I call him 'Your Excellency'?"

M. Martin answered: "Yes. Just say, 'How do you do, Your Excellency,' and after telling him that the Mother Superioress says that you are too young for her to give you permission to enter, ask him for the favor which you want."

"I am sure that he will let me enter the Carmel on my fifteenth birthday, especially since I look so grown up with my hair fixed like this, and my voice . . ." Thérèse instinctively lowered her voice.

On they rode. Deep down in her throat the "Little Flower of Jesus" practiced "But Your Excellency, if *you* will say that it is all right, the Sisters of the Carmel will be only too glad to have me there with my two sisters and the rest of the nuns. . . ."

The trees and the fences went quickly by.

Not more than three minutes had passed in the Bishop's house — and Thérèse knew that he too thought she was too young to become a nun. She tried hard not to start to cry.

Smilingly the Bishop's assistant whispered "I see diamonds." (He was referring to her eyes, already moist with gathering tears.)

The Bishop himself relieved the situation by asking: "Is it long since you first got the idea of entering Carmel?"

Thérèse replied promptly: "Yes, Your Excellency, a very long time."

The Bishop's assistant started to laugh saying: "Well now, it cannot be so very long; at most, it can be but fifteen years."

"It isn't much short of it," Thérèse answered, "for since I was three years old I have been desirous of giving myself to the good God."

For some time they talked but despite the fact that the Bishop and his assistant liked Thérèse very much, they would not give her permission to become a nun at the age of fifteen.

Thérèse was almost heartbroken. She did not know what to do. She looked at her father and he only smiled encouragingly. "My beloved king, whom can we see now, neither the Mother Superior, nor the priest, nor the Bishop will give me permission to become a nun at fifteen; whom can we see now?" A sudden light broke onto her flushed face. "The Pope, daddy, the Pope. Let us go and see the Pope!" Her face was triumphant. "He will certainly say it is all right. You'll take me to see the Pope, won't you daddy?"

M. Martin started to object saying that the Pope lived all the way over in Italy and . . .

On November the second they set off for Rome. They would have such a wonderful time, Thérèse knew. She, and her favorite sister Celine, and her father would be traveling for over three weeks! And besides that Thérèse felt sure that the Pope would allow her to enter the convent next Christmas!

Some of the friends of Thérèse thought that a mild fling in some of the great cities would change her mind about becoming a nun. But this was not so. Thérèse knew what she wanted. Yet she did have a splendid time with her sister and father. In Paris they caught glimpses of the glittering ballrooms, museums, and fashionable men and women; in Switzerland they saw the snowcapped mountains with their quaint villages and villagers; in Milan Thérèse viewed with wonder the white marble Cathedral with its statues numerous enough to form the population of Lisieux. Looking down from this Cathedral's lofty spire the whole city lay before her; the houses seemed to nestle up to the protecting walls of the house of God like chicks under the wings of the hen; little did she know that in one of those houses was the future Pope Pius XI, who would canonize and choose her as the patroness of his glorious reign!

Enchanting Venice did not fail to enchant her. Thérèse was so surprised to find that the only noise made in that city was the weird call of the gondolier and the stroke of his oar on the silent water. At Padua, after she and her father and Celine had seen the tongue of St. Anthony, they signed the visitors' register. At Bologna they saw the body of St. Catherine, whose face seemed still to bear the marks of the kiss received from the Child Jesus. Going through Pompeii the glowering Vesuvius loomed threateningly over them. Finally they came to Rome! Now, with the exciting day of her audience with the Pope at hand, Thérèse found interest in little else but talking about it. Even the magnificence of St. Peter's, the beauty of the Sistine chapel, the splendor of the Vatican, and the reminder of the triumph of the early Christians — the Colosseum — were not able to hold her attention for long. Wouldn't these three days ever pass?

They were waiting in line for their turn to see the Holy Father; Thérèse had a sinking feeling, even though she knew that the Pope would be very nice to her. She wondered whether she should talk to the Holy Father or not. For people did not do that unless they had something of great importance to tell. Celine was standing behind Thérèse and pushing her ahead gently. It was their turn next. M. Martin was just receiving the Pope's blessing. Thérèse looked at Celine wondering whether she should speak or not. Celine knew what she was wondering and whispered "Go ahead and ask him, don't be afraid, he's the Holy *Father*." Thérèse took a deep breath and knelt in her turn at the feet of the venerable white-clothed Pope Leo XIII.

She leaned over and kissed the huge ring which he held out for her to kiss. She was not afraid after all; so she raised her head and calmly said:

"Holy Father, I have a great favor to ask of you." As the great Pope lowered his kindly face toward hers Thérèse thought that his deep, dark eyes read her to the depths of her soul.

"Holy Father," she fearlessly went on, "in honor of your Jubilee, allow me to enter Carmel when I shall be fifteen years old." Thérèse was very naïve in the way she said "in honor of your Jubilee," and the Pope smiled, but just then one of the assistants stepped up and said: "Holy Father, this is a child who wishes to become a Carmelite. The matter is at present in the hands of the Superiors."

Thérèse's heart sunk for she knew that there was now only one thing that the Pope could say. And he said it: "Very well, my child, do as the Superiors will decide."

But Thérèse could not leave it go at that. She had been hoping and praying for this for such a long time. "Oh, Holy Father," she said, joining her hands and resting them on his knees, "if just you say 'yes' they will all agree."

Leo XIII then realized as he looked into her candid eyes that a great-souled girl was before him. With one of his thin white hands he raised her to her feet, and as she was getting up placed his other hand softly on her lips, and then slowly and solemnly raised it to bless her while saying: "Very good; you will enter if the good God so wills it."

Thérèse was crushed. She went out to her father who was waiting out in the hall and just looked up at him while tears streamed down her cheeks. M. Martin patted her on the shoulder, and she took heart for she knew that this was the game of ball she always played with the Infant Jesus. It was the game she had been playing ever since she was a little girl. In the game she always was to do the part of the ball, and she gave her Playmate to understand that He was not to regard her as an expensive ball — like one of those colored balls which some children carry about with them just to look at — but that He was to treat her as a cheap ball; that He might throw her on the ground, toss her about, or even pierce her to see what the ball was made of. In Rome He pierced His little toy, and finding what was within, He threw her on the ground, and, walking away, forgot all about her. It was hard. And she cried bitterly, but what could she do? She would play the game since she was the one who had promised; and so she said nothing. But Jesus was not to leave her forgotten for long.

Every day after they got home Thérèse used to wait for the mailman to come with some answer from the Bishop. The Pope had told her to wait. Three months passed; but still no answer. Thérèse prayed all the more. Finally, one day Thérèse heard the shrill sound of the mailman's wooden whistle. With a bound she was at the front door and tremulously received a letter from the Carmel and addressed:

"Mme. Thérèse Martin." At first she hesitated to open it; but then slipping her finger beneath the envelope's flap she excitedly pulled out the letter, read a bit, uttered a bated sigh of relief, then reread.

The Bishop, it stated, permitted her immediate entrance into the Carmel, but it was decided she must wait until after Lent. Hard as the delay was, Christ's little bride would only seek to be still more dear to Him.

Three months later M. Martin brought Thérèse to the convent. As they came up to the front door of the old convent of Carmel who should meet them at the door but Thérèse's older sister Pauline who took her in her arms as she entered.

The closing of the convent doors was not the end of living for Thérèse; in fact she knew it was just the beginning. At last she was where she had always wanted to be. She promised God that, for His sake, she would never do what she wanted to do, and always what others wanted her to do. He in turn would always do what she wanted Him to do. And that is just what happened. For instance, Thérèse liked things white; so on the day when she received her veil, even though the day was rather warm, God made it snow. So too with many other things. But there was one thing that she asked for again and again that she did not receive until after she died and that was — to be a missionary.

Her health was so delicate that her superioress would not leave her go to their missions in China or India. Instead she stayed at the convent to do God's will, and sang to Him at choir. Besides this she took care of the sick, cleaned the chalices, mended the vestments, and did other work in the sacristy, and even did some painting and writing. In fact the book the superioress asked her to write *The History of a Soul* (her own story) is a best seller of this century. In this book she tells of her way, "The Little Way," which is not hard for anyone to follow since it only means being a child with God.

When Thérèse, only twenty-five years old, was about to die, she said: "I will spend my Heaven in doing good upon earth"; and stated that we would know that she was really doing this by the fact that she would "let fall a shower of roses." And she has been doing just this. Today there is not a country in the world where some of her roses have not been received or where her help has not been felt and praised.

Thérèse, the Little Flower of Jesus, was a straightforward and loving girl. No wonder that God and all men love her so much that fifty-three years after she was born Pope Pius XI canonized her, and in generous fulfillment of her unfulfilled wish, made her special patroness of all missionaries.